ROLE-PLAY HANDBOOK

UNDERSTANDING AND TEACHING THE NEW REALITY THERAPY

COUNSELING WITH CHOICE THEORY THROUGH ROLE-PLAY

WRITTEN, COMPILED AND EDITED

BY

Brandi Roth, Ph.D.
433 N. Camden Drive, Suite 1128
Beverly Hills, CA 90210
(310)205-0615
www.associationofideas.com

Carleen Glasser, M.A.
22024 Lassen St., Suite 118
Chatsworth, CA 91311
(800)899-0688
www.wglasser.com

Role-Play Handbook
Understanding and Teaching the New Reality Therapy Counseling with Choice Theory through Role-Play
Written, Compiled and Edited
By Brandi Roth, Ph.D. and Carleen Glasser, M.A.

Copyright 2006 by Brandi Roth, Ph.D., Association of Ideas Publishing

All rights reserved. No part of this book may be reproduced or transmitted in any electronic, mechanical form by any means, including photocopying, recording or by any information storage and retrieval system without the prior written permission from the publisher. Permission to use forms is limited to personal use or for William Glasser Institute programs. Credit all forms to the authors. Not to be reprinted in any other publication.

First published in the United States of America in 2006
Association of Ideas Publishing
Brandi Roth, Ph.D.
433 North Camden Drive, Suite 1128
Beverly Hills, CA 90210 U.S.A.
310 205-0615
www.associationofideas.com

Library of Congress Cataloging-In-Publication Data
Roth, Ph.D., Brandi
Role-Play Handbook, Understanding and Teaching the New Reality Therapy, Counseling with Choice Theory through Role-Play
Compiled and Edited by Brandi Roth, Ph.D. and Carleen Glasser, M.A.
ISBN 0-9647119-2-3
1st Edition, P. cm Copyright Number
    1. Role-Play 2. Reality Therapy 3. Choice Theory 4. Counseling 5. Mental Health
      6. Relationship Counseling 7. William Glasser Institute

First Edition
10 9 8 7 6 5 4 3 2 1
Cover Photograph: Brandi Roth, Ph.D.
Cover Design: Bruce A. Clemens
www.associationofideas.com

ENDORSEMENTS

The core of teaching students to counsel with Choice Theory is practicing role-plays under the supervision of a faculty member of the William Glasser Institute. This handbook provides the structure needed for this instruction. It is unique in providing a collection of the talents of experienced successful instructors. It shows how innovative this teaching can be and gives students the hands on experience they need if they are to become successful counselors using the new Reality Therapy that integrates the teaching of Choice Theory directly into their counseling. This book should be a very useful addition to our teaching model.

William Glasser, M.D.

As the William Glasser Family of Helping Professionals, we are all stakeholders in the success of our Institute and the quality of our Instructors. This handbook, authored and edited by Brandi Roth and Carleen Glasser, assures the ever-widening faculty of Intensive Week Instructors and Practica Supervisors of a collection of some of our best teaching and learning standards. They have assembled several "rubrics" for moving our students in the direction of competency through quality to mastery. This is our universal direction if we share in the mission to "teach Choice Theory to the world." I believe a contribution to the compendium of creative ideas for the ethical practice of teaching Choice Theory is a professional responsibility. It is one I welcome. It has at its center the most effective way of helping people I have experienced in three decades of practice.

Suzy Hallock-Bannigan, RTC, CAGS;
Private Practice and Director of Counseling Services, Woodstock Union High School, Woodstock, Vermont and Liaison for the William Glasser Institute, Ireland

Acknowledgments

Thank you to all William Glasser Institute Faculty for your continuing caring and competent teaching of Choice Theory, Reality Therapy, Lead Management, Quality Schools and Public Mental Health ideas. We wish to express a special thank you to all the contributors to this role-play handbook. We made our best attempt to credit appropriately. Please notify us of clarifications or corrections. We welcome feedback and additional role-play activities from other faculty for future editions. This book would not be possible without your help.

A special thank you goes to Dr. William Glasser with whom we all share a vision for a better world through teaching and continuing to learn Choice Theory.

A special thank you to Carol Chandler for her untiring typing, graphics and editing, to Linda Harshman for her tireless editing and helpful advice and to Bruce Clemens for the cover design and creative editing.

TABLE OF CONTENTS

I	**INTRODUCING ROLE-PLAY**	**1**
	Introduction	3
	Some Suggestions To Instructors From William Glasser, M.D. For Teaching: *Counseling With Choice Theory, The New Reality Therapy*	5
	The New Reality Therapy: Counseling with Choice Theory	9
	The Art of Teaching Through Role-play	10
II	**GENERAL INFORMATION: POLICIES AND PROCEDURES FOR ROLE-PLAY**	**11**
	Role-play and the Art of Teaching Choice Theory, Reality Therapy, and Lead Management	13
	2005 Updated Institute Ethics, Role-play vs. Real Counseling	18
	Practicum Supervisor Forms	21
	Demonstration of Competence in Basic Practicum	22
	Demonstration of Competence in Advanced Practicum	23
	Advanced Practicum Activity	24
	Guidelines for Role-play	25
	Using Choice Theory in Counseling	27
	Configurations for Role-play Practice	29
	Role Definition for Role-play Practice	30
III	**CREATIVE APPROACHES TO THE ROLE-PLAY EXPERIENCE**	**31**
	Using Role-play To Counsel	33
	Role-play Techniques Using Reality Therapy	36
	Reality Therapy (WDEP)—Cycle of Managing, Supervising, Counseling and Coaching	37
	A Method for Role-play Practice Using Chart Talk	42
	Quality World Mapping	43
IV	**SELF-EVALUATION AND FEEDBACK APPLIED TO ROLE-PLAYS**	**47**
	Introduction to Choice Theory Group Planning Exercise and Self-evaluation/Planning Guide	49
	Group Planning Exercise Form	50
	Choice Theory Self-Evaluation/Planning Guide	51
	Facilitating Self-Evaluation and Giving Feedback	52
	Role-play Observation Form for the Purpose of Giving Feedback.	53
	Role-play Self-Evaluation Feedback Sheet	54
	Self-evaluation, Sometimes a Two-Step Process	55
V	**ROLE-PLAY STRATEGIES, ROLE-PLAY SCENARIOS AND ROLE-PLAY ACTIVITIES**	**57**
	A. Role-play Strategies and Developing Role-play Scenarios	**59**
	Role-play Using *Counseling with Choice Theory, the New Reality Therapy*	61
	The Choice Theory Cycle of Motivation	62
	Round Robin Warm Up Topics	63
	Role-play Scenarios	64
	More Role-play Scenarios	66
	Creating Role-play Questions Activity	67
	Creating Role-play Questions for a Lead Management Activity	68

Sample Questions Activity	70
More Questions for Role-play	71
Self-Evaluation Activity, Ways to Practice Role-play Elements	73
Matrix for Helping People Using Choice Theory; What Every Role-player Should Know	74
Example Role-play Feedback Form: Sample Questions	75
Role-play Feedback Forms	77

B. Focus Groups and Focus Group Activities — 79

Focus Groups: Using Focus Groups to Teach Choice Theory and Reality Therapy	80
How to Role-play a Focus Group in Practicum for the Purpose of Learning How to Facilitate One Activity	81

C. Practice with Relationship Role-plays: Counseling, Helping and Lead Management — 83

Four Wheels Game Role-play Activity	85
The Four Levels of Happiness	88
Role-play Using Problem Solving Framework	90
Collage Role-play	91
Role-play Relationship Stories and Obituaries from the Newspaper	92
Axioms of Relationships Activity	93
The Language of Choice Theory Activity	94
Relationship Tug Of War	95
Relationship Involvement Activity	96
Relationships and Our Habits Role-play Activity	97
Solving Circle and Role-play Solving Circle Activity	98
Role-play with a Need Strength Profile	99
Choice Theory Role-play Using the Shift Procedure	101
Choice Theory Role-play Using the Shift Procedure: Shoba's Counseling Situation	102
Choice Theory Role-play Using the Shift Procedure: Harold's Lead Management Situation	103

D. Quality World Activities — 105

My Quality World Relationship Activity	107
Sample Questions About My Quality World Picture Activity	108
Quality World Pictures: The "P" Principle	109
Role-play with Quality World Mapping Activity	110
Counseling Session Example of a Role-play Using Quality World Mapping	111

E. Quality School Activities — 113

Role-playing Class Meetings	115
The Art Of Questioning in Class Meetings	117
Class Meeting Group Activity	118

APPENDIX OF SUPPLEMENTARY INFORMATION — 119

Essentials of Choice Theory	120
Conditions for Quality in a Quality School as Applied To Role-play Self-evaluation	123
Choice Theory Glossary of Terms	124
Economics of Choice Theory Focus Groups as Group Therapy	125

ABOUT THE AUTHORS — 129

Brandi Roth, Ph.D.	131
Carleen H. Glasser, M.A.	132

RECOMMENDED RESOURCES AND REFERENCES — 133

I. INTRODUCING ROLE-PLAY

INTRODUCTION

Wonderful facilitators and mentors guided my journey to becoming a Basic Intensive Week Instructor at the William Glasser Institute. Many of these talented people had separately collected or developed creative materials to teach how to do role-plays. William Glasser was generous beyond imagination with his time and ideas. It struck me that what was needed was a single source where we could easily find the Role-play information and make it available to anyone who wanted to use it.

Carleen Glasser and I decided to create this handbook to collect these important works and to contribute our own works and ideas. This book is the result. We would like to add more Role-play activities to future editions. Please send Role-play materials that you would like to share with others who teach Choice Theory ideas. We would appreciate Word format materials e-mailed or mailed to us on a disk along with permission from the author to publish them in future editions

Role-play is central to facilitating the use of Choice Theory and Reality Therapy in counseling, managing and teaching. It has had a dramatic influence on my 35 year career as an educator and psychologist. Carleen and I hope you find this book useful. We hope to hear from you soon.

Brandi Roth, Ph.D.
www.associationofideas.com
brandiroth@yahoo.com

SOME SUGGESTIONS TO INSTRUCTORS FROM WILLIAM GLASSER, M.D. FOR TEACHING *COUNSELING WITH CHOICE THEORY: THE NEW REALITY THERAPY*

With the publication of the booklet, *Defining Mental Health as a Public Health Problem*, along with the specific information in my last nine books starting with Choice Theory in 1998, I have completed what I set out to explain when I wrote my first book, *Mental Health or Mental Illness* in 1961. From now on when I teach, lecture or write, I will explain that all the work I do with counselors, managers and teachers is aimed at teaching them to improve their own mental health by putting the concepts of Choice Theory to work in their lives.

For me, mental health, completely separate from what is now wrongly diagnosed in the DSM-IV as mental illness, is an important teachable entity that can lend itself to a wide variety of teaching techniques and counseling procedures. I assume that when our instructors teach they will follow my example but also feel free to use their own creativity to augment the way they teach my ideas. I believe that these ideas can be integrated into a variety of teaching techniques that could make them more accessible while remaining true to the basic principles of Choice Theory.

Some General Thoughts About Teaching Mental Health

Mental health could become a powerful unifying concept if we can explain it as a completely separate entity from mental illness as we do in the booklet. We should not be reluctant to use the term "mental health." By using it we have the opportunity to explain what it is and support our explanation with a free booklet. If psychiatrists or drug companies attack us for using the term mental health they will be placing themselves in the position of either standing for mental illnesses that they cannot prove actually exist or against mental health that has nothing to do with disease. We are on the high ground with mental health and that is where we should stand.

Some Suggestions for Teaching Mental Health Professionals to Counsel with Choice Theory

Starting with the first visit, the counselors we train would create warm, supportive relationships with their clients by being very careful never to use any external control in their counseling. They would also teach their clients that they are not mentally ill; they have no pathology in their brains, but may not be as mentally healthy as they would like to be. Our counseling will focus on helping them to get along better with the important people in their lives, to improve their mental health and become happier.

The Three Phases of the Counseling Component of Our Training Program

Phase One: The Effect of External Control on Relationships. Teach counselors why all their clients are having so much trouble getting along with some or even all of the important people in their lives. Essentially, the aim is to teach their clients that the difficulty that brought them into counseling is their use of external control psychology or, simply, external control. In this phase their clients are taught what external control is and how harmful it is to all their relationships.

Phase Two: Learning Choice Theory to Replace External Control

Teach counselors how to help clients replace the external control they have been using with Choice Theory or to use Choice Theory to escape from the external control that others are using on them. The most difficult concept to teach their clients is to continue to use Choice Theory as they deal with others even if the people around them continue to use external control on them.

Phase Three: Getting Comfortable Using Choice Theory

Teach counselors how to help clients practice what they have learned until they become comfortable enough to stop using external control. When they get to this point the counseling has been successful. They are now mentally healthier because they are living a Choice Theory life.

How Long Will This Take?

There is no predicting how long it will take clients to learn to integrate Choice Theory into their lives. But the more the counselor is able to integrate Choice Theory, directly or indirectly, into every conversation with the client, the sooner the counseling will be successful. To do this the counselor will continually point out to clients that they can only control their own behavior, and that any attempt to control anyone else's behavior will harm the relationship that is so important for mental health and happiness.

Key Concepts in the New Reality Therapy Counseling

1. Teach Clients to Focus on Present Behavior

Counselors will also teach the simple logic that explains that since all of us live in the present we can only control our present behavior. Therefore, all counseling takes place in the present. No one can control anything that happened in the past and we can only conjecture about the future. The past, no matter how good or bad, is over unless we talk about it right now in which case the past becomes a present but ineffective focus. Teaching clients to see how ineffective it is will move the counseling on to a more productive present.

2. Introduce the Basic Needs

An important need to focus on, and the need that motivates external control behavior, is the need for power. Teach that we cannot get rid of that need; like all five needs, it is encoded in our genetic structure. But the external control behavior itself is learned; it is not encoded in our genetic structure. Explain that the deadly habits and the caring habits are all learned. Counselors doing this make it clear to their clients what they are struggling with and how they can replace this struggle with new caring habits.

3. Introduce The Quality World

Teach the client that the Quality World is based on pleasure which means that pleasure itself is neither helpful nor harmful. But there are two kinds of pleasure: pleasure with people which is almost always helpful, and pleasure without people which is almost always harmful. Simply stated, pleasure with people is love and belonging; pleasure without people is usually an addictive behavior. Help clients explore their own quality world in this context. This is vital information and an important skill if we are to live a mentally healthy life.

4. Teach the Concept of Total Behavior: Thinking, Acting, Feeling and Physiology

Counselors should teach their clients that they can only directly control their own thinking and acting. They cannot directly control how they feel or what goes on in their bodies. But they can indirectly control what they feel and their physiology by changing how they think or act. Therefore, we suggest that counselors explain to clients that this is the reason why they do not focus on feelings and physiology separate from thinking and acting. But along with thinking and acting, a lot of the counseling will focus on how their feelings and physiology can change because this desire to change their feelings and physiology is very likely what brought the clients into the counseling office. Asking clients thinking and acting questions helps them to assess the direction they are taking their lives.

Effective Procedures That Help Clients Change

1. Begin by Asking Clients to Tell Their Story

All clients have a story and almost always want the counselor to listen to it and respond to it. As part of their story they usually tell you who they can't get along with but also add, "If that person would change, I'd be much happier." This is an early opportunity to teach clients that the only person's behavior they can control is their own. Point out that the best way to get along with other people is to put the relationship ahead of what each party wants. Teach them to use the golden rule instead of the external control rule they often live by which is "Do unto others before they do unto you.

2. Counsel with Choice Theory in Mind

Because they both know and use Choice Theory in their own lives, counselors always know what they are doing and why they are doing it when they counsel. How well or how quickly they can persuade, never coerce, their clients to put Choice Theory to work in their lives is up to their skill and their experience. When clients know what motivates their behavior they are more likely to change what they are doing to get what they want.

3. Ask Clients to Evaluate Their External Control Behavior

A valuable technique is to ask clients to evaluate if what they are choosing to do is helping their relationships. Or is it helping them to escape from the control of others who use these behaviors on them. Even if the client's evaluation is that what they are choosing is not effective, the counselor will still be very careful not to put any pressure on clients to commit to or act on their evaluation. To do that would be external control. However talking about the evaluation, offering suggestions, being supportive or showing appreciation for the potential success of the evaluation leading to their choice to change are all integral to effective counseling.

4. Look For Creative Expressions of the Ideas We Teach

In all these discussions counselors have the chance to be very creative, especially, to use humor to help the clients realize that external control behaviors are rarely effective. But we should also realize that external control, using it on others or trying to escape from it, is the creative theme of almost all humor. It is also the plot of most books, movies, plays, operas and other entertainment. To use stories and metaphor as examples to teach a counseling point in how or how not one chooses to live his or her life can at times be very effective. For example, the saying, "I've been rich and I've been poor and believe me rich is better" was the late comedian Joe E. Lewis's way to try to make the point that only rich people extol the virtues of poverty.

A final word

As stated, instructors are encouraged to use the most effective procedures their creativity can offer them when practicing the new Reality Therapy. Just be prepared to offer a Choice Theory explanation for anything you suggest but be patient and continue making the relationship with clients if they are not willing at first to accept your offer. Keep pointing out that the best evidence for putting Choice Theory to work in their lives is they will feel better. Until they feel significantly better the counseling is not over.

THE NEW REALITY THERAPY:
Counseling with Choice Theory

> Note: The new Reality Therapy focuses on unhappiness and addresses the use of external control psychology as a cause of that unhappiness in present relationships.
>
> The goal of the new reality therapy is not to "correct", "fix" or improve people's behavior. It is to make a relationship with the people you counsel and help them learn Choice Theory. With this information, they may choose to change their own behavior and improve their relationships by learning from the relationship you have created in the counseling environment. The procedures that lead to change are all learned through that need satisfying Choice Theory relationship.

Description of someone you would be counseling with Choice Theory®

SITUATION A

ENTER COUNSELING — UNHAPPY | Suffering the symptoms of disconnection | > | Physical & mental

⬇

Because of POOR RELATIONSHIPS | Basic needs unsatisfied | > | Quality world not matching their real world

⬇

Because of EXTERNAL CONTROL | The psychology of harming & destroying relationships | > | Making ineffective choices using the disconnecting habits

SITUATION B

EXIT COUNSELING — HAPPY | Enjoying a satisfying & connected life | > | No symptoms

⬇

Because of GOOD RELATIONSHIPS | Basic needs are satisfied | > | Quality world pictures met

⬇

Because of CHOICE THEORY | The psychology of creating and enjoying relationships | > | Making effective choices using the connecting habits

Carleen Glasser, M.A.

THE ART OF TEACHING THROUGH ROLE-PLAY

What is the purpose of a role-play? It is to teach counseling in a non-threatening environment. You are not actually working with real clients. You are working with simulated clients. It is not to accomplish therapy, it is to accomplish the learning how to do therapy. It is learning how to feel comfortable with the skills, to feel comfortable with the language. There is a certain language to counseling with Choice Theory and Reality Therapy; counselors need to know how to use that language and how to take external control out of your own approach to the counseling session. A role-play is demonstrating that you know how to model building a relationship without external control.

The position of The William Glasser Institute is that role-play is the main vehicle for instruction. William Glasser, M.D. has emphatically and clearly stated that role-play practice, not real counseling, is the focus of our training. It is through the process of role-play counseling that the participants receive their training and understanding of Choice Theory. The role-play practice is not designed as therapy to resolve a trainee's or the client's individual problem, but as a teaching tool.

This handbook is designed to add to the repertoire that instructors already have for teaching role-plays. The manual will present three separate areas of interest:

1. Review of the ethics, guidelines and procedures for role-play activities;
2. Types of role-plays and many practical suggestions to be used in teaching through role-play; and
3. The integration of Choice Theory to be used in the act of counseling.

This manual is a compilation of creativity by a number of outstanding instructors. It is our hope that it is a helpful tool to enhance our skills as instructors.

Brandi Roth, Ph.D. and Carleen Glasser, M.A.

II. General Information: Policies and Procedures For Role-Play

ROLE-PLAY AND THE ART OF TEACHING CHOICE THEORY, REALITY THERAPY AND LEAD MANAGEMENT

Robert Wubbolding, Ed.D.
John Brickell

ABSTRACT
Central to the art of teaching Choice Theory, Reality Therapy, and Lead Management is the use of instructor simulated demonstrations and participant practice. Explaining to participants clear guidelines, advantages, and limitation of this valuable tool enhances its effectiveness in skill building.

The William Glasser Institute has enshrined this tool in its official documents and publications used for teaching. However, participants need to understand that role-plays do not imply that Reality Therapy is "a quick fix" and that healing and better relationships occur as a result of brief interventions. Role-plays teach the process of Reality Therapy and Lead Management. They are not intended to demonstrate an immediate and permanent outcome. Rather, they teach the concepts of Choice Theory, the skills and techniques used in implementation, and relationship-building ideas, resulting in participant self-confidence, increased skill, and a sense of spontaneity.

Role-play, practice sessions, simulations, and demonstrations are phrases used to describe the art of implementing or operationalizing Choice Theory in training students. According to the *Programs, Policies & Procedures Manual of The William Glasser Institute (2003)*, a major portion of time is spent "practicing the Reality Therapy process in a variety of settings, with opportunity to role-play as both the helper and helpee." (p. 11).

Justifying the "how to" and explaining the delivery system, Choice Theory underlies the practice of Reality Therapy in counseling and psychotherapy, Lead Management in business, the Quality School education (Glasser, 1996) as well as the interplay of these various applications. It explains how the mind works as an internal control system by generating behavior for two purposes: to impact the outer world for want and need satisfaction and to send a message or communicate with it (Wubbolding): two purposes essential for building healthy relationships.

Below are described suggested guidelines, purposes, limitations and what observers can look for in order to derive maximum benefit from the experience.

Suggested guidelines for Role-play practice sessions:

1. Do not play yourself. In training weeks endorsed by The William Glasser Institute, participants simulate situations and issues with which they need help. They attend our programs for training, not for personal therapy. Experience has shown that they feel pressure to self-disclose if initially some participants bring into the open their personal problems. Based on the ethical principle of

informed consent, trainees do not attend programs expecting to self-disclose in the presence of a group. Wubbolding (1995) states, "Participants expect to use procedures. They are told that they will role-play, practice skills, and hear lectures. They come with the expectation of receiving training, not personal therapy."

2. Start with a real person or a composite. Counselors/therapists often choose to role-play their clients. Educators role-play their students, and business people their employees. An important guideline is that confidentiality is maintained. Instructors need to inform participants and make explicit the fact that even though role-plays might include considerable humor about ineffective client or student behavior, still the purpose of the simulation is to provide help for the client/student, not to demean them. If the "real person" role-played by the participant is identifiable, the details and process of the session remain in the training group.

3. No violence. In one intensive week, a participant played a very disruptive third grader by swinging her sweater at the helper hitting him in the face with a stinging blow. This simulation is unhelpful for learning CT/RT/LM/QS.

4. Play it as you feel it. Effective role-plays can illustrate movement from "Situation A" to "Situation B" (The William Glasser Institute, 2002). If the helpee in the role-play feels the urge to change his/her manner of communication from resistant to cooperative, the session can embody a valuable pedagogical lesson.

5. Stay in the role. Participants, on occasion, "run out of gas." The role of the instructor or helper is to help them stay in the role of client/student by leading the sessions and at times prompting the participant.

6. Facts are mutually agreed on. An effective guideline is "Whoever makes it up first, it's true." For example, if the helper says, "I talked to your mother last night," the helpee should not respond, "She died 5 years ago!!" Research has shown the effectiveness of Reality Therapy (Wubbolding, 2000), but it does not enable us to communicate with the dead!

7. Don't entertain the audience as a jokester. While humor helps people learn, participants who are exclusively concerned with their comedy routine in the role often detract from the value of the experience.

After briefly explaining these guidelines to audiences at intensive weeks, role-plays take on added value for participants. They frequently express their appreciation for structuring the session and providing for informed consent.

Purposes of Instructor Demonstrations

Because all behaviors serve a purpose, it is useful to unambiguously instruct trainees about the purpose of both role-play demonstrations by the instructor and practice sessions by participants.

The authors have found it useful to include in the first several hours, a demonstration session with a difficult, school-flunking, drug taking, behaviorally problematic (to others), resistant, alienated 15-16 year old student. In a systematic way, the helper discusses: belonging and its lack of effective satisfaction, i.e., how the student has chosen loneliness and alienation as well as occasions when the student chose more effective behaviors; power or achievement—by asking about the last time the person did something he/she felt pride; fun—by asking such questions as, "When was the last time you had a belly laugh?", "When was the last time you had fun without getting in trouble?"; freedom—by inquiring about recent contributing or altruistic choices made by the student.

This conversation, thorough or hurried, has several purposes, one of which is to demonstrate that it is possible to deal with highly negativistic and destructive behaviors indirectly by discussing their opposites. Even more instructive is the purpose of teaching the needs and quality world concepts to both a role-playing "client" and the workshop participants in a graphic and active manner. Thus, this role-play has a different purpose than other demonstrations.

More obvious purposes of subsequent instructor demonstrations include illustrating that the principles are applicable to any situation, showing the differences between environment and procedures, and emphasizing one or other of the components, e.g., exploration of quality world, discussion of current behavior, assistance in self-evaluating or plan making, teaching Choice Theory directly or indirectly, and dealing with unhappiness.

Participants' Practice Sessions

Students learn skills by using them in simulations using the above guidelines. However, they learn more than skills by role-play practice. They deepen their skill level, gain confidence, and increase spontaneity. Moreover, if behavior or experience controls perceptions, i.e., enriches the perceived world (Glasser 1985), then practice impacts our world view, imprints skills in the mind of the behavioral vehicle operator, increases the credibility of the CT/RT system, and provides opportunities for self-confidence building choices by participants.

Limitations of Role-plays

While role-play demonstrations and practice sessions have many pluses, there are limitations of which participants should be aware.

- People are not quickly cured. Participants attending training sessions drive their car more on "happiness highway" than on "misery lane," i.e., more in Situation B than in Situation A. Consequently, they often respond quickly to the effective use of Reality Therapy due to the fact that their skill in resisting is less developed than the real people they role-play. It is unrealistic to conclude, for example, that married couples with long term problems or a person grieving the loss of a spouse will easily choose ongoing relationship building behaviors in two or three contacts with even an empathic and highly skilled practitioner.

- Participants often ask how the helpee "felt" during the session—a fair but not always relevant question. Because the purpose of role-play is to teach and learn skills, they sometimes occur with less effective timing than they would in a real-time conference. In other words, at times the ordinary relationship-building conversation is omitted. Thus, the feelings of the "client" or "student" are not necessarily an accurate gauge for evaluating the helper's effectiveness.

Processing Role-plays

It is useful to explain that role-plays are like a videotape or DVD played at fast speed. They might seem to move faster than is possible with real clients or students. The helper can often demonstrate more ideas, skills, and techniques in a 10 minute role-play than in 30 or 40 minutes with "real" people.

Observers are instructed to look for relationship-building behaviors such as the ABC's or relationship tonics: attending, being present to the client/student, connecting with the person as a potential or actual success. These are the opposite of the toxic ABC's such as arguing, blaming, and criticizing which have created the present problems of the client or student (Wubbolding, 2002).

More characteristic of Reality Therapy are observations and feedback focusing on whether the helper facilitated a discussion of the quality world, level of commitment, and locus of control (W), total behavior (D), most significantly self-evaluation (E), and effective planning (P).

As Robert Wubbolding circulates to various groups at certification weeks conducting role-play demonstrations, he has developed a more advanced schema for observers in certification weeks. These can also be helpful in basic or advanced training programs.

1. Look for the unexpected. Is there any statement especially surprising to the helpee or to the observer? Look especially for non-verbal behaviors such as facial expressions or other body language.
2. Is there a pivotal point, a pivotal question resulting in a shift? Often, but not always, there are several points at which the client or student discovers that, "I am truly responsible for my behavior," "my excuses are getting me nowhere," "maybe this person does care about me and can help me."
3. Are there examples of indirect self-evaluation? Indirect self-evaluation techniques include story telling, often initiated by such comments as, "your situation reminds me of someone I met several years ago..." The helper then describes a person who worked through a similar problem with a satisfactory outcome. The student or client then ponders whether any of this anecdote is useful or provides an occasion for self-assessment.
4. Can any statement or question be transferred to another situation? Even though the role-play might focus on an elementary school situation, can questions be transferred to and used by probation officers, high school teachers, company managers, etc.? Self-evaluation questions are especially transferable. "Is what you are doing helping you?" "How realistic is it to be left alone and not to answer to anyone?"
5. What general principles emerge from the session? In the role-play with the recalcitrant teenager, the helper plays a teacher who informs the students that

he/she plans to set up study groups in the class. After allowing a choice for one person to team with, the teacher retains the authority to select another person for the team and informs the student. Principles emerging from this session are the effort to democratically involve students in decision making and the ultimate responsibility of teachers to maintain their position of authority.

Summary

Role-play demonstrations and participant practice sessions occupy a central place in training. They provide credibility for the instructor and for the instructional content. They also serve to help participants increase their skills as well as self-confidence in implementing Reality Therapy. Their usefulness increases when participants understand and implement helpful guidelines.

See also **Recommended Resources and References**

(The first author is Director of Training for The William Glasser Institute. The second author is Director of the Center for Reality Therapy in the United Kingdom)

Permission to reprint granted
Robert Wubbolding, Ed.D.
International Journal of Reality Therapy,
Spring 2004, Volume XXIII, Number 2, Page 41

2005 UPDATED INSTITUTE ETHICS: ROLE-PLAY VS. REAL COUNSELING

(Participants being themselves rather than their clients or students in practice training sessions during intensive weeks.)

Robert E. Wubbolding, Ed.D.
Director of Training: The William Glasser Institute.

Updated December 2005. The original was published in the *Journal of Reality Therapy*, Vol. XIV, No. 2, Spring 1995, pp. 83-85.

Please note: updated comments are italicized.

In an effort to increase the quality of training The William Glasser Institute has placed more emphasis on the pivotal place of role-play in the certification process. The additions below reflect and summarize these refinements in institute policy.

Many ethical and professional issues have been discussed in these pages during the past several years, i.e. issues related to consultation (Wubbolding, 1991a, 1991b), suicide (Wubbolding, 1987, 1988, Hallock, 1988), informed consent (Wubbolding, 1986), and dual relationships Wubbolding, 1993). Recent discussions within the Institute indicate the need to elaborate on how ethical issues relate to the certification process. Please consider the following case:

> Lee is a workshop participant in a basic intensive week. In setting the stage for practicing the CT/RT principles, the instructor asks Lee to be a client for a role-play demonstration. Lee describes his own personal problem and decision and freely agrees to ask for help. The instructor agrees that Lee can be himself in the demonstration. Role-play is thus not utilized in this case.
>
> Lee describes feelings of depression as a result of being a single parent with the responsibility of raising three pre-teenage children. The spouse had suddenly asked for a divorce and moved out of state with a much younger companion of the same sex. During the session the client becomes quite emotional, showing anger, rage, and subsequent embarrassment.
>
> The participants feel the responsibility of assisting Lee who later expressed profound regret at having consented to "real therapy." The instructor believes the participant needs extra attention and spends several evenings counseling this "client." At the end of the week, Lee states, "all is well now. I'm OK. I'm really OK. I've put the entire problem behind me." The other participants are not sure.

QUESTION: What is wrong with the above picture?

ANSWER: There is almost nothing right with this scenario. Many ethical issues are involved in the highly questionable events that occurred.

Institute Documents:

It is the position of The William Glasser Institute that practice sessions conducted in training programs include role-play. Throughout the training process from basic intensive weeks through instructor programs, role-play is the main vehicle for instruction (Programs, Policies, & Procedures Manual, *2003 pp. 9-15*). For example in the Advanced Week, "the participant is expected to participate more actively than during the Basic Intensive Week. There is more emphasis on role-playing and the processing of the role-plays" (ibid., *p. 12*).

Additionally, Dr. Glasser has emphatically and clearly stated that role-play practice, not real counseling, is the focus of our training. He stated if "one person were to commit suicide, it would be a thousand too many" (1994).

Thirdly, the Advisory Board of the Institute has unambiguously endorsed the position that practicing skills in Institute programs includes role-play practice, but not "real therapy" (1994).

Fourthly, at its March 12 - 13, 2004 meeting, the Advisory Board restated and reemphasized the singular importance of role-play demonstration and participant role-play practice at every level of training and endorsement. The purpose of role-plays is to provide opportunities for participants to increase their skills and to provide a structure for instructors to teach Choice Theory as well as the environmental and procedural components of Reality Therapy. Thus role-play constitutes "the heart of the program" (Wubbolding, 2004, p. 19). The central place of role-play in institute training does not exclude other teaching tools. Activities in which participants apply the principles to their own lives in a non-threatening and enjoyable manner are clearly congruent with Institute policies.

Multiple Relationships:

Elsewhere I have summarized a major ethical issue in the helping professions (1994). I wish to argue here that "real counseling" in intensive weeks extends beyond dual relationships into an even more complicated multiple relationship. An instructor who demonstrates Reality Therapy with "real counseling" establishes a therapist-client relationship on top of the instructor-trainee relationship. This dual relationship is rendered more complicated when the purpose of such a session is described. Is the primary responsibility of the instructor to counsel the client or to instruct the participants? In any counseling session, the helper's primary responsibility is the client. However, the other participants/observers have not contracted with the instructor or organizer to observe someone else resolve personal problems.

Informed Consent:
In attending Institute training programs, participants expect to be trained to use the procedures. They are told that they will role-play practice skills, hear lectures, etc. They come with the expectation of receiving training, not personal therapy.

Moreover, because the relationship between trainer and trainee is distinct from that of therapist/client, it can be argued that it is one of **supervision** or consultation. The American Counseling Association describes the **relationship between supervision and counseling: "If supervisees request counseling, supervisors provide them with acceptable referrals. Counselors do not provide counseling services to supervisees" (Section E, 1). In describing the consultation relationship, The Canadian Counseling Association states that the focus of the relationship is on issues to be resolved not on the persons presenting the problem** (Section D, 2).

Uncovered Issues:
In entering a therapeutic relationship, the client needs to understand that issues might emerge that include a beginning, middle, and an end, i.e., disclosure, discussion, and closure. Thus if participants agree to receive "real counseling," to be themselves, they should be informed that the full process of counseling cannot occur in the short period of an intensive week.

Moreover, experience has shown that some individuals seem to freely consent to "real counseling" without realizing the many implications and consequences. They often express regret or confusion at a later date. Or, as in the case of Lee, they minimize the over-inflation of the feeling wheel of their behavioral car or even deny it. Thus the outcome of this "counseling" is that clients can be worse off than before they received such insufficient help.

In the voyage to higher quality the Institute has attempted to stay on course and to practice what it teaches. The documents clearly describe beliefs about the content of training. Participants' informed consent is based on the expectation that these beliefs are modeled and made specific in the training programs and that our professional relationships are clear and unambiguous.

PRACTICUM SUPERVISOR FORMS

DEMONSTRATION OF COMPETENCE
FOR BASIC AND ADVANCED PRACTICUMS

Role-play practice is a central part of the practicum experience. These Demonstration of Competence forms are provided for faculty to assist participants in keeping a record and journal of their experiences with participation and role-plays. The form includes role-plays with familiar clients, unfamiliar clients, feedback and self-evaluation and how they apply Chart Talk or Choice Theory ideas in the role-play.

The following competencies are organized in two documents which can be used in practicums. For Basic Practicum the handout is recommended as a useful tool but not required for successful completion. Participants give feedback that it is helpful as a guideline for the content of the practicum and the expectation of competence.

The Demonstration of Competence in Advanced Practicum is requested of all Advanced Practicum participants in order to be recommended for Certification Week. Participants have found the form valuable and have appreciated the opportunity to record and document their experiences in practicum. The forms have been useful for the practicum supervisors to complete recommendations for participants to the next level of training. Both were developed by Carleen Glasser, M.A. and Brandi Roth, Ph.D.

DEMONSTRATION OF COMPETENCE IN BASIC PRACTICUM

The following competencies will be demonstrated by each participant in the Basic Practicum in order to be recommended for **Advanced Week**.

PARTICIPANT'S NAME: _____

COMPETENCIES: (CO-VERIFICATION BY BASIC OR ADVANCED PRACTICUM SUPERVISOR)

                                          FACILITATORS INITIALS_____ **Date:** _____

1. ROLE-PLAY WITH A FAMILIAR CLIENT
    Play the counselor to a familiar client in a fifteen minute role-play demonstrated to the group, dyad, triad, and/or round-robin
Notes:_____

2. ROLE-PLAY WITH AN UNFAMILIAR CLIENT
    Play the counselor to an unfamiliar client in a fifteen minute role-play demonstrated to the group, dyad, triad, and/or round-robin
Notes:_____

3. FEEDBACK
    Demonstrate feedback to another participant's role-play
Notes:_____

4. SELF-EVALUATION
    Discuss with the group your strengths and areas in need of improvement
Notes:_____

5. CHART TALK
    Run a role-play through the loops of the chart
Notes:_____

Remember to include the following in your participation: Refer to Dr. Glasser's books and ideas; knowledge of CT/RT/LM; teach using Choice Theory; demonstrate group management and handling of professional responsibilities and ethical issues.

ATTENDANCE DATES	LOCATION	FACILITATORS	PAYMENT MADE CK#/CASH
1			
2			
3			
4			
5 (Optional)			
6 (Optional)			
7 (Optional)			
8 (Optional)			

Carleen Glasser, M.A. and Brandi Roth, Ph.D.

DEMONSTRATION OF COMPETENCE IN ADVANCED PRACTICUM

The following competencies will be demonstrated by each participant in the Advanced Practicum in order to be recommended for **Certification Week**.

PARTICIPANT'S NAME:_____

COMPETENCIES: (CO-VERIFICATION BY ADVANCED PRACTICUM SUPERVISOR(S))

              FACILITATORS INITIALS_____ Date:_____

1. ROLE-PLAY WITH A FAMILIAR CLIENT
   Play the counselor to a familiar client in a fifteen minute role-play demonstrated to the Practicum group
   Notes:_____

2. ROLE-PLAY WITH AN UNFAMILIAR CLIENT
   Play the counselor to an unfamiliar client in a fifteen minute role-play demonstrated to the Practicum group
   Notes:_____

3. FEEDBACK
   Demonstrate feedback to another participant's role-play
   Notes:_____

4. SELF-EVALUATION
   Discuss with the group your strengths and areas in need of improvement
   Notes:_____

5. CHART TALK
   Run a role-play through the loops of the chart
   Notes:_____

6. PRESENTATION PRACTICE
   Prepare a 15 to 20 minute in length Certification Week Presentation and practice in front of the group
   Notes:_____

Remember to include the following in your participation: Refer to Dr. Glasser's books and ideas; knowledge of CT/RT/LM; teach using Choice Theory; demonstrate group management and handling of professional responsibilities and ethical issues.

ATTENDANCE DATES	LOCATION	FACILITATORS	PAYMENT MADE CK#/CASH
1			
2			
3			
4			
5 (Optional)			
6 (Optional)			
7 (Optional)			
8 (Optional)			

                 Carleen Glasser, M.A. and Brandi Roth, Ph.D.

ADVANCED PRACTICUM ACTIVITY

PURPOSE: This is an Advanced Practicum Role-play activity for the Development of the Certification Presentations.

DIRECTIONS: Have the participants fill out the following form then have the group discuss their plan and get feedback from each other.

Designing an Activity for Certification Week

The activity presentation for Certification Week is designed to demonstrate your competency to understand and to teach others the basic principles of Choice Theory the New Reality Therapy and the Total Behavior Chart.

The Choice Theory competencies and practicum experiences you want to demonstrate:
_____
_____
_____

How does the group participate in this activity: (Are the directions clear?)
_____
_____
_____

What materials will you use?
_____
_____
_____

What can the participants take away with them so they can use this activity in their work or Choice Theory experiences?
_____
_____
_____

Debriefing the group:
What did you like about this activity?
What did you learn by participating in this activity?
What questions would you like to ask?
Are you closer to developing your presentations?

Clarann Goldring, Ph.D.

GUIDELINES FOR ROLE-PLAY

I. Establish the Counseling Environment.

In what specific ways did the counselor create a supportive environment? (Friendly? Caring? Non Critical? Open?) In what ways did the counselor help the client gain a sense that he/she could make changes to improve life?

II. Procedures That Lead to Behavior Change.
1. In what ways did the counselor help the client focus on present behavior?
2. Were questions of the components of total behavior used to help the client understand that total behavior is chosen?
3. Did the counselor help the client make the connection between the present unhappiness and the present chosen behavior?
4. In what ways did the counselor help the client to clarify what he/she wants? Were the wants and needs developed and clarified well before the client was asked to evaluate their effectiveness?
5. Was the WANT connected to WHAT ARE YOU DOING TO GET WHAT YOU WANT connected to HOW EFFECTIVE IS YOUR PRESENT CHOSEN BEHAVIOR IN GETTING WHAT YOU WANT?
6. Watch for stray wants or evaluative questions if you seek to have the client see the connection.
7. How did the counselor use visual analogies and questions to get into the client's perceived and quality worlds?
8. How well did the counselor focus on the client's perceived and quality worlds rather than what the counselor believes the client should see or want? In other words did the counselor work in the client's head or his own? Remember in some settings it is necessary to convince the client that it may be need fulfilling if a particular behavior is changed. (In schools and in management this is often the situation).
9. Did the counselor help the client understand that the only behavior anyone can control is his/her own?
10. How did the counselor get a commitment from the client to look at some more effective behavior choices?

III. Incorporating Self-Evaluation toward Quality in Practicing

1. Discuss in group what a quality role-play or practice looks like.
2. Decide what your quality role-play will look like.
3. Determine name, age, situation of client and if voluntary or involuntary so you can plan an agenda if you are managing as well as counseling.
4. To self evaluate use the following guidelines as conditions for quality.
   A. Was it useful? Quality is never destructive to individuals or to society.
   B. Was it the best you can achieve at this time?
   C. Quality always feels good; did it feel good?
   D. Quality can be improved. How can it be improved upon?

5. Feedback from an observer is seen as co-validation. This should be made in terms of the two components of counseling as presented by William Glasser, M.D.
    A. In what manner did the counselor in role-play establish a counseling environment?
    B. Discuss how the procedures which led to behavior change were employed.
    C. Suggest an alternative approach.
1. The role-playing client may choose to comment.
2. Based upon the information from the feedback and from self-evaluation, make your own plan for improvement in your role-playing. If you were managing did you discuss quality, were you non-coercive and did you allow of self-evaluation?
3. Continue to discuss quality in role-playing.

IV. Making a Plan.
Was the Plan:
Need satisfying? Sufficiently simple to be attainable? Realistic? "ACTION" rather than "NO ACTION"? Both specific and repetitive? Success focused upon the activities of the client rather than contingent upon others?

V. Assuring Success of the Plan.
Did the counselor make certain that the client agreed that the plan had a chance of success? How did the counselor help achieve a commitment to the plan?

Adapted by Brandi Roth, Ph.D.

USING CHOICE THEORY IN COUNSELING

Georgellen Hofhine introduces Choice Theory in Counseling by giving participants this handout. Participants have found this approach to be helpful as a way to focus on what is happening within the thinking of the client rather than what the counselor is doing. With practice in practicum the skills improve. Reading this before starting a role-play helps participants focus from the total behavior in the counselor's head to the total behavior in the client's head.

Using Choice Theory in Counseling

Understanding and using this process is based upon a thorough knowledge of Choice Theory as developed by William Glasser, M.D. Focus is upon the client's behavior rather then upon technique you employ. When you counsel using the two components of Reality Therapy, i.e., the establishment of the environment and the procedures leading to change, you may anticipate certain behavior changes for the client. Your artful skill and sensitivity will direct your pace and questions if you focus on the client rather than technique. Be friendly as you listen, remembering this is not a police interrogation; it is a friendly conversation. It is the relationship you create and maintain with the client that encourages and supports his/her more effective choices. You have avoided any hint of external control.

Two Components of Counseling

1. **Counseling environment**
   As you create a supportive environment the client will begin to choose to feel safe and move toward trust. He may even begin to learn as he relates as a friend. There is no external control in this environment and it feels good.

2. **Procedures that lead to change**
   With your questioning your client will begin to understand that behavior is chosen and that he can choose only his own. Of course, no one else can control others but you have not coerced. Your questions have gently allowed him to search pictures in his quality world. When he perceives that his present behavior is chosen he may also see that his present misery or unhappiness is related to his present chosen behavior. He may begin to understand that he can make a different choice. He can envision how he wants his life to be and is free to make more effective choices. He glimpses his own control over these choices and his life.

   The client evaluates his present behavior as having minimal chance of getting what he wants. This evaluation by the client is the core of Reality Therapy and the first circumstance for making a behavior change.

   Your client has recognized that his present behavior is chosen, and evaluated that what he is doing does not have a reasonable chance of getting what he wants. NOW the two of you can explore other choices. When he perceives that there are other choices he will be working toward the second circumstance for making a behavior change.

Ah, here's the rub. Even after self-evaluation the client may find it difficult to make changes that you and he have identified. But you will not give up and with your continued support he may choose to make more effective choices.

Georgellen Hofhine

CONFIGURATIONS FOR ROLE-PLAY PRACTICE

Whole Group Role-play: In this method, the leader plays the part of a client or a member of the group plays the counselee. The whole group works with the client by firing out questions randomly. The whole group represents one counselor. This gives those people who feel comfortable asking questions the opportunity to do so and the rest who are not ready to participate a chance to hear the questions and think of things they would have said if they were ready.

Round Robin: Similar to the whole group, the Round Robin has the participants each take a turn counseling one client by asking two or three questions. Then pass to the person next to them to take over. Each person in the group should have a turn. The client remains the same. Often the facilitator plays the part of the client.

Fish Bowl: In this method half the group sits in a circle surrounded by the rest of the group in the outer circle. The group in the center circle will be observed role-playing by the outer circle and given feedback. This can also be practiced by the whole group in a circle with only one counselor and one client in the center of the fish bowl being observed role-playing.

Dyads or Pairs: This method involves two people doing a role-play, one acting as the client, the other the counselor, and then switching roles at the end of each role-play.

Triads: This method involves three people doing a role-play, one playing the client, one the counselor and the third the process observer. At the end of each role-play the participants rotate roles until each one has had the opportunity to play all of the roles.

10-15 Minute Audio or Visual Recording of a Role-play: This method involves the participants recording themselves doing a role-play acting as the counselor. Each recording is then played back in practicum and listened to for its effectiveness in procedures that lead to change and integration of Choice Theory. Alternative approaches to the recorded role-play can be discussed and or then replayed by participants in dyads, triads or round robin so that the original role-player who made the recording can see the different directions the role-play could take. This approach is time consuming for the participant to prepare and does not allow for instant feedback but it does give the participant doing the role-play time to review the tape several times and to write or record a self-evaluation of his or her performance to present to the group.

Carleen Glasser, M.A.

ROLE DEFINITION FOR ROLE-PLAY PRACTICE

The following terms help the participants identify roles they might play or role-play practice:

Client
- Presents a problem
- Realistic but not difficult
- Purpose is to facilitate the "helper's" learning
- Stay in the role
- Don't tell "helper" what to do
- Don't use real life situations in which confidentiality could be compromised
- No personal issues

Helper/therapist
- Counselor—has no agenda
- Manager—has agenda
- Stays in the process
- Uses Reality Therapy process
- May offer ideas/suggestions, but always acknowledging that the client has the choice
- Creates environment
- Self evaluates

Feedback/Sharing Role
- Offers feedback as information, not "e value ation"
- No criticism—criticism leads to defensiveness
- Constructive criticism is an oxymoron
- Offers suggestions as "something I might have tried is…"

Facilitator
- Defines roles to group
- Demonstrates the process
- Makes sure people stay in roles
- Structures environment, creates "safety net"
- Sets guidelines such as time
- Asks "helper" if there's something he/she wants to work on specifically
- Facilitates self-evaluation
- Reviews the process
- Asks if "helper" wants feedback
- Adds to feedback
- Supports, encourages, does not criticize, coerce
- Teaches from the role-play

Pat Robey, M.A. Facilitating a BPSP

III. Creative Approaches To The Role-Play Experience

USING ROLE-PLAY TO COUNSEL

Role-play is a guided way to tell a story to reach objectives and receive feedback from an independent neutral person. Therapy clients report that role-play in counseling is very helpful to them. Without this process, many people continue to repeat ineffective behaviors. Exchanging perceptions through role-play expands clients' understanding of how they are perceived, how they act and how they influence success or failure. With role-play, clients become more energetic and creative faster than in any other form of counseling. A counselor builds coping skills and insight. This process leads a person through the three stages to problem solving.

1. What happened (as the client perceives it)?
2. How does the client feel now? What is the client thinking now? What is the client doing now? How is the client's body responding? (Total Behavior)
3. What is the client planning to do next? Does the client have a plan for a solution (move in a new direction and/or change of behavior)?

Clients avoid difficult conversations. It is challenging to sort through thoughts about difficult topics, feelings, or actions. It is easier for the client to avoid them or to ignore them. Avoiding topics can lead to misunderstandings, unnecessary worries or behaviors that result in unhappy relationships. Role-play practice provides a safe vehicle to rehearse approaches to resolution and to practice facing dilemmas. Practicing thinking and feeling can lead clients toward an action plan. Open communication is best approached in one or more of the following negotiations: Mutual agreement after each person presents his perception, his needs, and his wants. This simple agreement usually occurs in relationships where trust and goodwill are high. More often there is a need to agree to disagree, or to postpone the discussion, or to compromise or engage a third party to help mediate.

FIVE PROBLEM-SOLVING TECHNIQUES IN RELATIONSHIPS

4. Agree on the solution or approach to the dilemma. This can only be done if the relationship is committed, and trust and goodwill in the relationship is high. Resolving the dilemma with an agreement may mean the problem is solved and there is no need to continue with the next four steps.
5. Agree to disagree. If a discussion leads to an unresolved dilemma, a decision to agree to disagree may be the best solution.
6. Postponement. If a solution or resolution must be reached, agreeing to discuss it later after each person has given more thought to it may be the best interim solution. Agree to a follow-up time.
7. Compromise. There are three approaches to compromise: First, one person acquiesces to the other person's viewpoint. Second, there is a combination of the two viewpoints. Third, an independent viewpoint is agreed upon.
8. Mediation or arbitration. Settlement with a mediator who facilitates agreement or an arbitrator who decides.

REVERSE ROLE-PLAY TECHNIQUE

Role-play has a very important place in counseling. Its use with clients in psychotherapy and its use by teachers with students provide a dialogue that far surpasses a conversation or a monologue. Role-play gives the client or student the opportunity to speak the words that person has been thinking, or feeling or experiencing physiologically. Everybody has a story to tell about the layers of experience they have had. Telling a story relates what happened, the way they felt, how they acted and their body response to the experience. Total Behavior (Physiology, Feeling, Thinking and Acting) gives a framework for processing the experience and making a picture of the perceptions. Discovering how the needs of the Quality World picture can be met, (i.e., what the person wants) can be better understood with role-play. Role-play also helps a person think with an expanded viewpoint and with creativity. Role-play is presented from a myriad of perspectives. The ethics of role-play are well defined by the William Glasser Institute policies. Dr. Glasser has provided a recent update of his view of teaching Reality Therapy and Choice Theory with role-plays in this book.

Reverse role-play is effective at adding insight and leading to a new plan. The approach has many forms. The counselor offers to play the role of the client, and the client plays the role of a family member or other person who the client is reluctant to approach.

Example: Counselor, "Would you be willing to have me role-play you and you will play your (example, wife)?"
Jane (played by the counselor)
Matthew (played by the client)
Jane: "I'd like to tell you some thoughts I've had on my mind. I would like to let you know I am sad when you over drink and I am unable to converse with you."

Feedback from clients about reverse role-play has included the following comments:
"When I heard you play me, I understood for the first time that the things I think can be said without fear."
"I heard a way to say what I think. Before, I had no words."
"It gave me the courage to speak my mind."
"Now I can express what I want in my way with my words; I have a better sense of what I want to say."
"This gave me a greater compassion for my ... (partner, friends, student)."
"Playing my partner and listening to you play me opened my mind to other choices I would never have thought of."
"Learning about differing view points has been enlightening."
"I feel more empathetic about my (wife's) view."
"You talk about a toolbox of ways to handle situations. I have more in my toolbox."

From the therapist's viewpoint I can shortcut understanding my client with reverse role-play. The feedback conversation after reverse role-play is of great value. Questions like the following enhance understanding and the experience:

"How accurate was my depiction of what you need and want?" "What more did you want me to ask or clarify?" "What ideas occurred to you about what you would like to communicate or do?"

Living life by paying attention to needs increases effectiveness in choices. Role-play increases awareness faster than any other technique. To live well in the present is empowering. Role-play integrates the Choice Theory language and builds skills of relating effectively. Role-play provides a powerful vehicle for advancing learning. It enhances understanding of how the learning has been integrated and processed.

A follow up meeting to review how a role-play was applied to a real life situation is important. In that session self-evaluation and reflection are emphasized and questions like; "How effective were you when you communicated your needs and wants?" "What did you apply from the role-play?" "What did you add that emerged in the actual exchange?" "What would you like to practice today?" A traditional role-play rather than a reverse role-play usually follows these follow-up questions after the earlier role-play.

Brandi Roth, Ph.D.

ROLE-PLAY TECHNIQUES USING REALITY THERAPY

1. Reality Therapy Question Formulation. The group leader is the client. The group forms into pairs or teams (e.g., experienced and non-experienced). Each team's job is to formulate a question for the client, thinking out loud so the rest of the group can hear. Teams are asked to give a rationale for the questions they consider. Group members can briefly give some input by asking questions about the thinking process. This process needs close facilitation by the group leader to be effective. Participants are not used to thinking out loud or creating a counseling process with another person, but this can be a very useful learning experience. This is best used during advanced training.

2. Teaching Process Feedback and Self-Evaluation. Group is organized into pairs for a one-on-one role-play. After a stated time of 10-15 minutes, time is called and participants are told not to discuss the session. The person playing the counselor moves over one seat and the new client helps the counselor self-evaluate. The idea is for the counselor to be asked questions about his/her role-play without the other person having seen the session. This provides a pure process of self-evaluation without the possibility of feeling criticized. In addition, the person asking the questions is practicing the questioning process without the concern of being in the role of counselor. Participants who have not yet learned the questioning process can use a prepared question sheet. Otherwise, this is best if used during advanced training.

3. Teaching Participants to ask Open-Ended Questions (as opposed to closed or leading questions)
      a. Start questions with *how, what,* or *why.*
      b. Insert some part of the client's last answer into the questions.
      c. Connect it to a *want.*

This is best used after a role-play when the content of the session can be used for illustration and example.

4. Teaching strategy
Beginning counselors often express concern that they can't think of the next question to ask. When a client attributes something to someone else, (e.g. "My teacher thinks that..." My mother wants me to...," "My boss says...") the next question should always be: "What do you think...?", "What do you want...?" or "What would you like to say...?" This technique illustrates the concepts of Choice Theory by demonstrating that the client is in control, his opinion is important, and it helps sort out what he wants.

5. Never Ask Why!
For many years faculty were trained not to ask clients for reasons for their actions as part of the Reality Therapy questioning process. However, Dr. Glasser in one of the many refinements of his teaching over the years now says that asking "why" is one of the best questions except when you are dealing with irresponsible behavior. Why someone wants to attend college could be an effective question using Reality Therapy since it helps explore the quality world. Asking, "Why are you using drugs?" would not be recommended because it implies (even if unintended) that a good reason would be acceptable or understandable. Thus, the rule of thumb is why is a good question to use except when dealing with irresponsible behavior.

Al Katz, M.S.

REALITY THERAPY

Robert E. Wubbolding, Ed.D.

I. Description of Treatment: Environment and Procedures
II. Theoretical Bases: Choice Theory
III. Empirical Studies
IV. Summary
    Further Reading

GLOSSARY

Choice Theory The underlying principles of Reality Therapy that emphasize behavior as chosen for the purpose of satisfying inner genetic instructions or needs.

Environment The therapeutic atmosphere or climate that serves as the basis for specific interventions.

WDEP The delivery system of Reality Therapy, signifying **W**ants, **D**irections and Doing, Self-**E**valuation, and **P**lanning.

Founded by William Glasser, M.D., Reality Therapy has its roots in the work of Alfred Adler, who emphasized that human beings are social in nature and that behavior is goal centered. Glasser extended his early ideas to include genetic instructions or human needs as sources of human behavior. Accordingly, human beings originate their own behavior. It is not thrust on them by their families, their environment, or their early childhood conflicts. Rather, behavior is seen as chosen. In the early stages of its evolution, the formula for Reality Therapy was described as involving eight steps. Used widely in therapy, counseling, corrections, as well as in education, Reality Therapy attempted to avoid coercion and punishment and teach inner responsibility. Its current formulation as a delivery system, developed by Dr. Robert E. Wubbolding in his books **Using Reality Therapy** and **Reality Therapy for the 21st Century**, is summarized with the letters WDEP. Its use now extends to self-help, as well as management, supervision, and coaching employees.

Describing the root of human strife as flawed relationships, Glasser has provided a theoretical and conceptual blueprint for addressing human conflict. Wherever human relationships are improved, productivity increases in the workplace, families remain intact, students achieve, and organizations achieve their goals and function more humanely.

I. DESCRIPTION OF TREATMENT: ENVIRONMENTAL AND PROCEDURES

Figure 1 presents an outline of the delivery system for Reality Therapy. Establishing a safe atmosphere or environment provides the basis for the more specific interventions known as procedures. As in any therapy the therapist listens to clients' stories presented in their own words and seeks to become part of their inner discourse. In the language of Choice Theory the therapist becomes part of the clients' quality world (i.e., someone who is capable of providing needed help). The procedures are the specific tools for helping clients clarify and prioritize their wants, evaluate their actions and self-talk, and finally, make plans for effective change. The "Cycle of Managing, Supervising, Counseling, and Coaching" is applicable to many relationships and is used in many settings where human relationships are paramount: teaching, therapy and counseling, consultation, management and supervision. Moreover, Reality Therapy employs several strategies common to all counseling theories.

Also, although the environment is the foundation upon which the procedures are built, there is no absolute line of demarcation between them. Thus "Build Relationships" is both environmental and procedural. Nor is the "Cycle" a simplistic lock-step method to be entered unwaveringly at the same place with every patient. People using Reality Therapy in their human interactions, enter the "Cycle" at various points. Although a therapist generally establishes a friendly, warm relationship before employing procedures that lead to change, helping clients evaluate their own behavior and make plans often occurs early in the therapy process.

Finally, because Reality Therapy is used in corrections, in classrooms, and in many relationships besides therapy, specific helpful and hurtful and behaviors as well as attitudes are described under environment such as "don't criticize" and "don't encourage excuses."

A. Environment

The word "environment" implies an effort on the part of the therapist to establish an atmosphere in which the patient can feel safe, secure, and motivated. As shown in Figure 1, hindrances to establishing a trusting, helpful, safe environment include arguing, bossing, blaming, criticizing, demeaning, colluding with excuses, instilling fear, and giving up easily. In consulting with parents, educators, managers, and others, therapists often teach the ineffectiveness of such choices.

Opposite the ineffective environmental behaviors is a wide range of helpful, effective, and facilitative suggestions leading to a trusting atmosphere. These include attending behaviors, use of paradoxical techniques and metaphors, listening for themes related to procedures, skill in demonstrating accurate empathy, and helping clients find choices even amid their feelings of depressions, perceptions of oppressions, and lack of opportunities to fulfill their own needs.

B. Procedures: The WDEP System

The environment serves as a foundation for the effective use of procedures that lead to change. They are not a series of recipes used mechanically. Rather they are a network or a system defined by the acronym WDEP. Therefore, depending on the presenting and underlying problem, the therapist extracts from the system appropriate components for application.

1. W: Explore Wants, Needs, and Perceptions

Essential to the process of change, as well as facilitating the relationship, is a clear determination and definition of clients' wants or desires. They are asked to describe current pictures or to insert firmly in their "quality worlds," exactly what they want. Using the analogy of wants as pictures, it is evident that clients often have blurred wants. They are unclear about what they want, so when they are asked, "What do you want from your job, from your spouse, from your parents, from your children?" the answer is, "I don't know" or "I'm not sure." An adolescent often wants "my parents off my back" or "to be left alone" but is unable to provide a detailed and unambiguous description of this desire. Consequently, the reality therapist helps clients clarify and define wants, which is the process for the beginning of effective action on the part of clients.

Another part of the W is the exploration of clients' perception or viewpoint. The therapist asks the parent of a child, "How do you see your son or daughter?" in the case of a severely upset child, the parent might answer, "I see a lazy, rebellious, surly, uncooperative, and ungrateful child." Of course, such questioning is combined with an exploration of wants, for example, "What do you want from him or her?"

To the workaholic parent of a child, their therapist could say, "I see your 18 hour days not as a 'rendezvous with destiny' but as a collision course for you and your children." To the parent of the teenager, the counselor might say, "I see your son or daughter as a person who needs a compliment for even a minor success or change." In the practice of Reality Therapy, therapists take an active but non-authoritarian role, and see themselves as partners in the process of change.

2. D: Doing (Total Behavior)

Behavior is composed of four aspects: doing, thinking, feeling, and physiology. A popular misconception is that Reality Therapy neither deals with nor allows for a discussion of feelings and emotions. This erroneous perception is perhaps derived from the accurate statement that in Reality Therapy the action aspect of the behavioral system is emphasized (although not to the exclusion of the other components). Still, there are two important aspects to this procedure: exploration of overall behavioral direction and specific actions or choices.

The therapist encourages clients to be specific in the discussion of behaviors, such as exploring a specific segment of time: a day, a morning, an hour, an incident, or an event. Although it is important to examine the overall direction of total behavior, direction will change only with small measurable changes made one at a time. Thus, therapists help clients become a television camera describing specific rather than typical events.

3. E: Self-Evaluation

If the entire process of environment and procedures is a cycle, the procedures appear as an arch with its keystone self-evaluation. This component is a prerequisite for change in human behavior. No one chooses a more effective life direction or changes a specific behavior without making at least a minimal self-evaluation that the current course of action is not advantageous. Effective change rests on judgments related to total behavior, wants, perceptions, and other aspects of the client's life.

The term "Evaluation" has a meaning in Reality Therapy that is different from its meaning in other theories. In Reality Therapy the procedure described here is not an assessment evaluation or "clinical diagnosis." Rather, it is a series of value judgments, decisions and changes in thought made by the client. In the restructuring of thought, clients come to the conclusion that their life direction is not where they want to go, that a certain exact and specific current behavior is not useful or not helpful, that what they want is not attainable or helpful, that a perception is not effective, and that a future plan of action represents a more need-fulfilling behavior.

In the "Cycle," evaluation comprises an axis that closely connects procedures and environment. Reality therapists help clients evaluate their own choice systems (wants, behavior, perceptions) as well as devote considerable effort toward the evaluation of their own specific professional behaviors and generalized competencies.

4. P: Planning

If evaluation is the keystone of the procedures, planning is the superstructure or the goal. A plan of action is crucial to change. It can sometimes be complicated and sometimes simple. There must always be a plan. People, who go through life without some sort of long-term plan are like ships floundering without rudders. This procedure is the easiest to bring about if the therapist has prepared the way by the effective use of the more subtle procedures and environmental components already described. Nevertheless, if the plan is to be effective, it should be characterized by as many as possible of the following qualities summarized by the acronym SAMIC^3.

S=Simple: The plan is clear and not complicated.
A=Attainable: Realistically doable rather than grandiose and impossible.
M=Measurable. An effective plan is precise and exact.
I=Immediate. Implementation immediately after or even during the therapy session is desirable
C=Controlled by the planner. A plan should not be contingent on the behavior of another person.
C=Committed to. The reality therapist elicits a firm commitment.
C=Consistent. The plan should be repeated.

The WDEP system should be seen as a unit, a system in which one component affects the others, and so, the subsystem W, D, E, and P are not isolated steps that must be followed one after another. Rather, it is more appropriate to extract from the system whatever component is most relevant at the moment. Through listening, practice, and supervision, a user of Reality Therapy can develop a sense of where to start and how to proceed through the "Cycle."

II. THEORETICAL BASES: CHOICE THEORY

The practice of Reality Therapy is based on Choice Theory. Previously lacking a theoretical framework for Reality Therapy, Glasser employed the relatively obscure principles of control system theory to explain its effectiveness, and extended the theory to provide a basis for clinical practice by presenting a detailed explanation of human needs, total behavior (actions, thinking, feelings), perceptions, and inner wants or "quality world," the phrase used to describe our specific wants and intense desires. Control system theory is based on the principle that living organisms originate their behavior from the inside. They seek to close a gap between what they have and what they perceive they need at a given moment. This discrepancy, called a "perceptual error," sets the behavioral system in motion so as to impact the external world. Human organisms act on their external worlds to satisfy needs and wants. They gain input from and generate output toward the external world. Because of the emphasis on inner control and especially because of the emphasis on behavior as a choice, the theory was renamed Choice Theory in 1996.

III. EMPIRICAL STUDIES

The question is often asked, "Does Reality Therapy work? Is it effective?" Dr. Robert Wubbolding has provided an extensive summary of research conducted on its efficacy. Investigators have found an increase in the self-esteem of clients and a greater realization of the meaning of "addict," a significant reduction in the rate of recidivism with juvenile offenders, and a complete re-socialization of a large number of prison residents, all of whom received Reality Therapy treatment.

Much research has been conducted in schools measuring the effects of counselor and teacher training in Reality Therapy. Teaching students to self-evaluate their behavior and their work has resulted in a drop in teacher referrals for discipline and other problems.

A sampling of research in a variety of settings illustrates the wide use of this system. Participants in training workshops leading to certification represent psychology, social work, counseling, classroom teachers, administration, corrections, geriatrics, and other disciplines. Although there is ample research to demonstrate the viability of Reality Therapy as a therapeutic method, more is needed. Wubbolding recommends that close attention be given to the quality of training provided for therapists, teachers, and others who use the system so that the genuine use of Reality Therapy is measured. Also, more studies measuring outcome (i.e., change in behavior) are needed.

IV. SUMMARY

Reality Therapy, formulated as WDEP, is a practical and jargon-free system based on Choice Theory. Its philosophical principles include the belief that people choose their behavior. It is not imposed from early childhood or by external stimuli. Therapists help clients define their wants, evaluate their behaviors as well as their wants, and makes plans for future change.

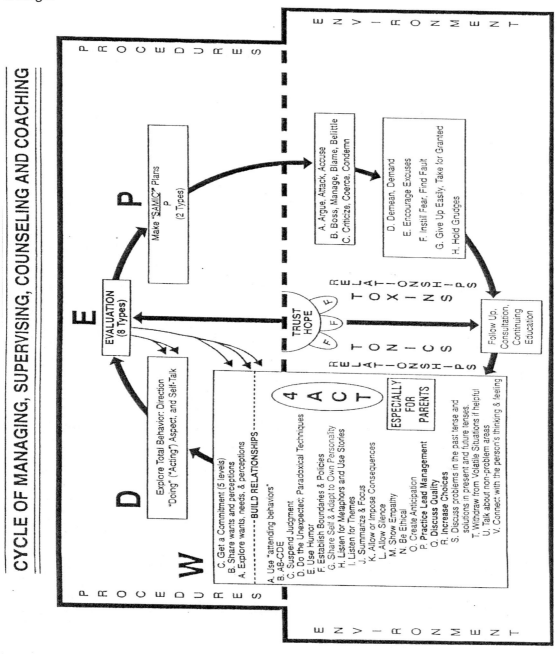

Figure 1

Developed by Robert E. Wubbolding, Ed.D. from the works of William Glasser, M.D.
Copyright 1986 R.E. Wubbolding, Ed.D., 15th Revision 2006

A METHOD FOR ROLE-PLAY
PRACTICE USING CHART TALK

 Enter from any direction

Discuss and ask about

Quality World

Pictures based on Basic Needs

Sample Question: What would you see yourself having if your needs were all fulfilled in your relationship?

Discuss and ask about present, total

Behaviors / Choices

Sample question: What are you Thinking? Doing? Feeling? What is your body telling you about your relationship?

Focus
On relationship
Not on symptom

**TEACH CHOICE THEORY
Using its four components**
Always ask:
Whose behavior can you control?

Discuss and ask about quality world pictures not matching real world perceptions, the

Comparing Place

Sample Question: How does what you have match with what you want in your relationship?

Discuss and ask about reorganizing choices, new directions, utilizing

Creativity

Sample Question: What can you do that will get you more of what you want in your relationship?

Carleen Glasser, M.A.

QUALITY WORLD MAPPING

In the late 1980's many of us Instructors were teaching the importance of "internal reference perceptions." During those years, Dr. Glasser had taught us the concept that the notions or "pictures in the client's head" are perhaps "the most important part of the client's life." Because these pictures are stored in a special part of the memory, and because that storage procedure begins to happen shortly after birth (and some may argue even before birth), this world of pictures becomes very special. In the early days of the evolution of what has now come to be called Choice Theory, we called this "The Internal World" or the "All-We-Want-World." That world, which may exist in our imagination or longings, represents the world in which we would really like to live. From the start, William Glasser has called this special world our personal "Shangri-La."

But in the early 1990's Dr. Glasser read Robert M. Pirsig's book *Zen and the Art of Motorcycle Maintenance.* Sometimes called "*An Essay on Quality*," this particular book asks the questions, "What is good?" and "What is not good?" The notion of Quality emerges almost as a non-thinking process, and because definitions, by their very nature, are constructed by formal thinking and then I suppose thinking about thinking (which some people refer to as "meta-cognition"), the definition of Quality is elusive. In his musings about this question, both philosophical and scientific, Pirsig suggested that Quality cannot be well defined. He then suggested that a real demonstration of Quality can happen for us by "showing that a world without it cannot exist as we know it." Pirsig also reasoned that at the moment of "pure Quality...there is no subject and there is no object. There is only a sense of Quality. ...At the moment of pure Quality, subject and object are identical." Pirsig continued: "A thing exists if a world without it can't function normally." He proceeded to subtract quality from a description of the world as we know it.

Dr. Glasser has always given attribution for his inspirations. These have included Dr. William Powers for *Control Theory*, W. Edwards Deming for concepts about evaluation, management and systems, and Robert Pirsig for giving us the vocabulary for "Quality." By 1996, Dr. Glasser had renamed and better defined "The Quality World."

I found Robert Pirsig's demonstration utterly convincing and I immediately understood why Bill Glasser assigned the term "Quality World" after I tried Quality World mapping with my clients and my students. I read to them from Pirsig and asked them to create an example, a slice, from their Quality Worlds. We would use large poster board and begin to proceed through many categories. Because some Quality World Pictures seem permanent to us, an indelible part of who we are as people, I sometimes would invite people to write in ink Quality World Pictures which they believed would remain with them always. I always wrote the names of my children: Brook and Benjamin. But many times, Quality World Pictures could be less definite, even transitory, as people grow and change. For most pictures, we fastened post-its onto the poster board. Post-Its now come in multiple sizes, and so people can now refine those maps even more by having small pictures, bigger pictures, and Very Big Pictures! Because the color of Quality on the Big Chart is yellow, I used yellow Post-Its. As Pirsig would proceed to subtract Quality from a description of the world, we used those very subtractions to chart our worlds.

The first quality, Pirsig claimed, would be the Fine Arts. There really isn't any point in hanging a picture on a wall if an unadorned wall looks just as good. Why would any of us travel to hear live music if a recording on a scratchy machine could sound just as sweet to our ears? The Arts are all about what is good. So our first categories would be the visual arts (and I would write Walter Osborne, Monet, Manet, Courbet and other Impressionists, Leonardo da Vinci, Michelangelo, Paul Henry (Irish painter), John Singer Sargent, and I would even write "my pink roses oil painting" which is unsigned but treasured by me. When people ask you in an Involvement Exercise to identify what you might enter a burning house to rescue, right up there on my list after pictures of my children and my pets, I would rescue those pink roses! And, for Music, there is always Van Morrison, U-2, Chopin, Debussy, Sean Tyrell, Rachmaninoff, Siebelius: my friend Hilary Scanlan would never miss a moment to write or see Christy Moore. Some of us would include Norah Jones, Katie Melua; lots of us would still include Frank Sinatra no matter how that dates us. In Vermont, the group Pfish would be a big Quality World Picture. I cried with Carmel Solon once in Dublin when I heard *"Dublin in the Rare Old Times"* and *"Grace."*

Literature is another category which traditionally yields results, especially in the Republic of Ireland where so many students are well read in the canon. James Joyce, Brendan Kenelley, Patrick Kavanagh, and William Butler Yeats were put sometimes on Post Its, sometimes written in permanent ink. Playwrights and authors abound: Sean O'Casey, Shakespeare; in the last couple of years, Alexander McCall Smith. Best, most memorable films ever seen, sculptors, and other artists and craftspeople of all kinds emerged on the maps. Pirsig said if there were no Quality, comedy would vanish too. And sports or games of any sort would just disappear---no one would want to play, scores would be meaningless, audiences would not attend them. My students and clients would list all the sports which were in their Quality Worlds: golf, hill walking, and horseback riding were frequent.

Though this exercise felt slow and it could stretch well, I found it one of the very best ways to teach The Quality World. At the end of the Mapping, students would share a Picture (or two or three) with a partner in dyads, and invariably, people found commonalities. The SOS Peer Counselors at Woodstock Union High School do this exercise every year at their annual training retreat, and one graduate, Michael Leonard, a salutatorian, included his map in his graduation address at commencement. Other students have wanted to laminate their "Worlds," and when I cautioned a student and said, "But you will grow and change, and so will your Quality World," she said, "But I want to always remember who I was when I was in high school and this says it all."

Dr. Glasser has called the Quality World the "core of our lives" and our "direct motivation." He has written convincingly and with disclosure about his own. We know that Miss Sheehan is in his. So is his computer, and if you carefully read each book's dedication, you will note the people who occupy a special place in his Quality World. Things and Systems of Belief are there: the Sunni and Shiite

Muslims have sharp disagreements about their Quality Worlds. Most negotiations and conflict resolution have much stronger prognosis for successful outcomes if the Quality Worlds of each party to the conflict are known and deeply understood. Some of us are very particular about our Quality World Pictures---our French toast has to be a certain thickness, for example---and the more particular and highly defined the pictures, the more we may have to struggle to get them met. The counselor's awareness of one's own Quality World is one reason to seek Consultation frequently. There are ethical issues about imposing our values on our clients, about understanding the systems of values which define our cultures, and the morality of held pictures which must necessarily caution us as helping professionals to know our clients and to know ourselves at this level of understanding called "The Quality World."

Suzy Hallock-Bannigan, RTC, CAGS

IV. Self-Evaluation And Feedback Applied To Role-Plays

INTRODUCTION TO CHOICE THEORY GROUP PLANNING EXERCISE AND SELF-EVALUATION/PLANNING GUIDE

The next two forms are useful in teaching individual self-evaluation and for working with teams or organizations in plan-making for change. The questions on both forms are based on the four Choice Theory components from the chart: basic needs, quality world, total behavior and creativity which include evaluation and planning. Having individuals or groups fill out the forms then discuss what they wrote leads to learning the questioning techniques used in effective role-play to practice counseling with Choice Theory—the new Reality Therapy

GROUP PLANNING EXERCISE

In working with groups or organizations like schools and businesses it is useful to help them self-evaluate the system in order to begin the process of improving it toward quality.

CHOICE THEORY IDEAS	QUESTIONS FOR THE GROUP OR TEAM TO BRAINSTORM	GROUP PLANNING PROCESS ANSWERS BY CONSENSUS
BASIC NEEDS: • SURVIVAL • BELONGING • POWER • FREEDOM • FUN **QUALITY WORLD:** • IDEAL • PICTURE/VISION	• What is our vision, ideal picture? • What do we need to be more effective? • What are our goals? • What do we want to be able to do that we are not doing now? • If we had what we want, what would that look like?	**Our vision:**
CHOICES OF BEHAVIOR: Internal vs. External Control	• What is our current practice? • What have we been doing so far to get what we say we want? • Which of our goals have we achieved? • In what areas have we lived up to our ideal picture or vision? • Is our behavior internally or externally motivated? Are we using external Control?	**Our choices**
ASSESSMENT OF OUR CHOICES	• Is our current practice working? • Is what we are doing, how we are behaving, getting us closer to or further away from achieving our goals? Our vision? • If our behavior is full of external control, is it working for us? • Is there room for improvement in what we are doing?	**Our assessment:**
CREATIVE PLANNING	• If what we are doing could use some improvement, what is it and what can we do to improve it? • What plan can we make today, based on Choice Theory, that each of us would be willing to follow and take responsibility for sharing?	**Our commitment**

Carleen Glasser, M.A.

CHOICE THEORY SELF-EVALUATION/PLANNING GUIDE

CHOICE THEORY IDEAS	QUESTIONS YOU CAN ASK YOURSELF	FILL IN YOUR ANSWERS HERE, KEEPING CHOICE THEORY IN MIND
BASIC NEEDS: • SURVIVAL • BELONGING • POWER • FREEDOM • FUN **QUALITY WORLD:** SPECIFIC PICTURES OF PEOPLE, THINGS, SYSTEMS OF BELIEF LINKED TO THE NEEDS	• What do I need in this situation? • What specifically do I want that I'm not getting? • What do I see in the real world that is not matching my quality world picture? • What is my ideal picture?	**Wants:**
TOTAL BEHAVIOR: ACTING > I CAN CONTROL THINKING > I CAN CONTROL FEELING > INDIRECTLY PHYSIOLOGY > CONTROLLED BY WHAT I CHOOSE TO DO	• Which component of my total behavior have I been focusing on to get what I want? • What choices am I making now to get my needs met? • In my relationships with others, what am I choosing to do? Are we moving closer or further apart? • Am I using any of the seven deadly habits?	**Behaviors:**
MY ASSESSMENT OF THE CHOICES I HAVE BEEN MAKING	• Whose behavior can I control? • Is my behavior working for me? If not... • I what I am doing now going to get me more or less of what I want? • Am I using external control in my relationships with people? Is it helping the relationship? • Am I happy or unhappy with my current relationship?	**Assessment:**
TRUSTING MY CREATIVITY, I CAN MAKE A PLAN TO BE MORE EFFECTIVE	• What can I do today that will improve my relationship? • If what I am choosing to do to get what I want is not working, what else could I do that might be more effective? • What is my plan? • Can my plan be started today and is it dependent only on my own behavior?	**Plan:**

Carleen Glasser, M.A.

FACILITATING SELF-EVALUATION & GIVING FEEDBACK

Feedback should only be given AFTER the helper has had a chance to self-evaluate, and only if he/she wants feedback. Feedback should be positive, to encourage repeating strengths. Give suggestions for alternate approaches only if the helper wants them.

Suggested questions to facilitate self-evaluation:
Ask of "helper:"
- What did you hope to accomplish in this role-play?
- How did you create a safe environment for your client?
- What was effective?
- Was there an area in which you would like to improve?
- What would you do differently next time?
- Do you want information form me, the "client" or the observers? If so, what kind of information would be helpful?

Suggested areas from which to offer feedback:
Ask of "client:"
What was most helpful to you?
Did you feel an internal "shift?" If so, when?
What questions would you have liked to be asked?

Observations from Process Observer/Reporter (be specific, use examples from the role-play.)
- Regarding the environment, I noticed that you…

Were friendly	Addressed behavior
Were a good listener	Empathized
Appeared competent	Accepted no excuses
Didn't give up	Kept the responsibility on the client

- Regarding the process

I thought the following questions were effective…
You identified the client's want by…
You gathered information about the client's behavior…
You asked the client to evaluate when you…
You facilitated the client's plan…

- I have suggestions for alternate approaches if you are interested in hearing them…

Receiving Feedback

Always remember: Feedback is only someone's perception of what they have seen. Feedback is information. Take feedback in at the knowledge level, place a value on it based on what is important to you, and make changes that will help you grow.

Patricia Robey, M.A.

ROLE-PLAY OBSERVATION FORM
FOR THE PURPOSE OF GIVING FEEDBACK

Keeping Choice Theory in Mind

Directions:

To be used during the role-play by the process observer.
Write only the **questions** the counselor asks in each category below. Do not write what the client says. Use this form to help you give feedback to the person role-playing the counselor.

QUALITY WORLD PICTURES	PRESENT BEHAVIORS	PLANNING FOR CHANGE

Carleen Glasser, M.A.

ROLE-PLAY
SELF-EVALUATION FEEDBACK SHEET

Introduction:

After the role-play is over each person who participates in a role-play and plays the part of the counselor should be given this feedback sheet to fill out. It will help them to self evaluate. It will also give them an opportunity to share with the group their thoughts about what they liked about their participation and what they want to improve. It gives them an opportunity to use this information to ask the group that observed them to give them feedback based on these questions that they are asking themselves.

Participants:

THE FACILITATOR OR PRACTICUM SUPERVISOR

THE PERSON PLAYING THE CLIENT

THE PERSON PLAYING THE COUNSELOR

THE OBSERVERS

What I liked about my participation was…

What I still want to improve is…

What I still want to know is…

What I will do to find out is…

My role-play scenario ideas for the future are…

My level of comfort and plan to continue growing through role-play is…

Adapted from Training by Jean Seville Suffield

SELF-EVALUATION, SOMETIMES A TWO-STEP PROCESS

Self-Evaluation became a focus of learning and exploration at the recent Basic Week Instructor Training in Livonia, Michigan, led by Al Katz, M.S. and Patricia Robey, M.A. We found ourselves struggling with the clarity of our evaluations and the specific focus of our feedback. Dialogue revealed that we were sometimes focused on our own total behavior and confusing that with our perception of the effectiveness of the activity. We developed a two-step process of self-evaluation, illustrated by these concentric circles and sample questions.

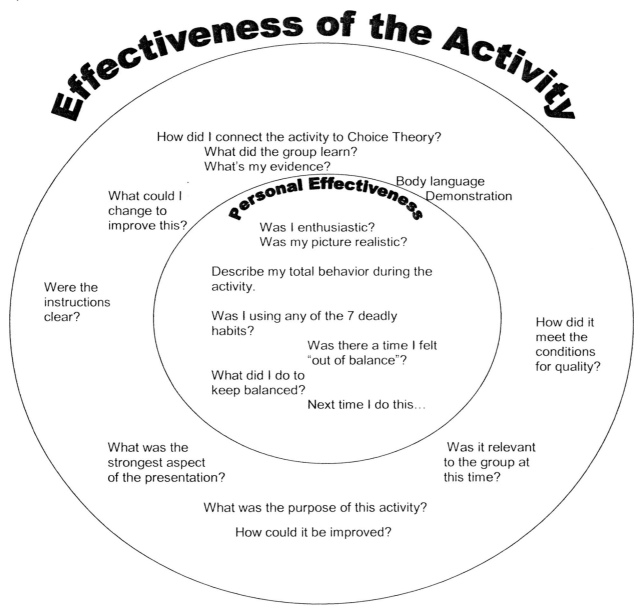

We had the most difficulty self-evaluating when our scales had been tipped during the activity. At these times, doing two separate self-evaluations clarified the process for us. The outer circle represents our perception of the effectiveness of the activity. The inner circle represents our effectiveness in managing our own behavior. Both are important in learning to provide quality instruction.

Peter Driscoll, M.Ed., Judy Comstock, MS, and Julian Pierce

V. Role-Play Strategies, Role-Play Scenarios And Role-Play Activities

A.

ROLE-PLAY STRATEGIES AND

DEVELOPING ROLE-PLAY SCENARIOS

ROLE-PLAY USING *COUNSELING WITH CHOICE THEORY THE NEW REALITY THERAPY*

PURPOSE: To become comfortable discussing the role-play process by defining roles and practicing questions

DIRECTIONS: In his book *Counseling With Choice Theory*, Dr. Glasser gives examples of how he has worked with various clients in his private practice throughout the years. After reading the book, select a counseling session scenario and role-play the same client using an alternative approach in a direction that you might like to go and have the group brainstorm various alternative approaches to that client using the practicing of counseling with Choice Theory that is taught in practicum, advance trainings or faculty trainings.

For instance if you select chapter 9 the client called Maureen, (Maureen wants to stay married even though she is in a very problematic marriage.) How would you teach, counsel, or work with Maureen. What direction could you take? First of all if you were seeing her for the first time or if perhaps you were seeing her after a session with Dr. Glasser. Examples of ways you could use Maureen to explore relationships would be:

- Feeling isolated from the relationship or from the family
- A relationship with substance abuse as a problem
- How to find alternatives when the family advice is: just get a divorce
- What strategies have you learned through training that would benefit a client like Maureen?
- Find ways that you could teach Maureen Choice Theory that would be applicable to her relationship problem.
- How would Maureen benefit by participating in a Choice Theory focus group?

Carleen Glasser, M.A. and Brandi Roth, Ph.D.

THE CHOICE THEORY
CYCLE OF MOTIVATION ACTIVITY

PURPOSE: The purpose of this activity is to help people create questions for the role-play that will facilitate the client's self-evaluation process.

DIRECTIONS: Make up new questions for each block on the chart. For instance what do you HAVE that you really WANT (in the HAVE block)? What do you WANT in your quality world that either is or is not in the real world (in the WANT block)? Is there a match between what you WANT and what you HAVE (In the MATCH block)? What are your CHOICES (in the CHOICES block)? Do you want to change what you HAVE? Do you want to change what you WANT? There are lots of different questions that can be made up to ask in a role-play based on this Cycle of Motivation Chart.

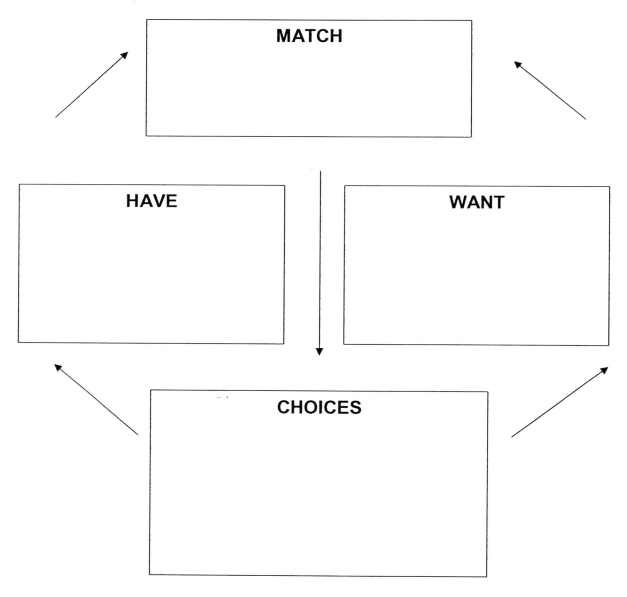

Carleen Glasser, M.A.

ROUND ROBIN WARM-UP TOPICS ACTIVITY

PURPOSE: Start the day with warm-ups to role-play experiences. As preparation for eventual role-play practice, get participants to begin to feel comfortable talking in the group. This activity provides Ways to introduce participants to each other, as a welcoming activity, helps make connections and sets a cooperative spirit for the day.

DIRECTIONS: Invite the group to go around with the list below and interview each other on the following topics:

- Introduce yourself

- State your expectations

- Describe your prior knowledge of Choice Theory

- Talk about ways you use Choice Theory in your relationships or your work

- Tell a little known fact about yourself

- Tell a short story about your name

- Describe something you do well

- Describe an activity that you plan that will facilitate growth and change.

- Describe ways to change an attitude, belief or area of thinking you are stuck in (the transfer of one energy to another creative effort.)

- Have you had a defining moment in which you applied knowledge of Choice Theory

- Do you have a story in your real life that is an example of applying Lead management, Choice Theory or Reality Therapy? Tell a short vignette.

Ideas from faculty and developed by Brandi Roth, Ph.D.

ROLE-PLAY SCENARIOS

PURPOSE: To give everyone some ideas about scenarios they could role-play.

GUIDELINES:
If you are playing the counselor you may ask other group members if they would be willing to play one of the situations outlined below.

If you are the client remember to ask if it is acceptable if you play a particular role. If a situation is uncomfortable, avoid it. Do not play yourself or a situation close to you. Also, try not to play "stump the therapist." Keep in mind that the objective is for everyone to improve their skills using Reality Therapy and have fun as you learn.

DIRECTIONS: Select a scenario from the list below and role-play with a partner.

Work Issues
- I've been a stockbroker for 20 years and now I think I want to teach...
- I am a woman who wants to return to work against the wishes of my husband.
- I am afraid to approach my boss about an important work-related issue.
- I hate my job.

Parenting Issues
- I want to stop yelling at my kids.
- My child's room is always a disaster zone.
- I dislike my daughter's boyfriend. He's a poor student, wears black all the time, and has excess body piercing.

Personal Issues
- I have no energy. I'm neglecting some of my chores and responsibilities and I've tried everything. You've got to help me. "Do you think I have something seriously wrong with me?"
- I want to lose weight, quit smoking, or cut back on drinking.
- How can I create more "me time"?
- I feel miserable because I did not achieve a job, promotion, award, position in a social club, another date with love interest, athletic achievement, etc.
- I was offered a great new job but I have to leave my love interest, kids, parents
- How can I regain the trust of a friend, partner, family member, etc.
- How can I get over my fear of flying, leaving home, crowds, authority

Marital Problems
- Client and spouse are locked in conflict over:
  - Where to spend vacation
  - Where to spend retirement
  - How to discipline the kids
  - What to do about aging parents
  - What to do with large inheritance they just received
  - One partner going back to work

- Jealousy
- Drinking problems
- Not wanting to be married anymore

School Issues
- ❖ A student:
    - Is put in time-out for arguing with the person he sits next to.
    - Does not come in promptly after recess.
    - Is often tardy.
    - Skips classes and/or school often
    - Is giggling about something and not paying attention to the lesson
    - Seldom finishes an assignment in class and never finishes a homework assignment.
    - Does not like physical activity and tries to get out of recess or P.E.
    - Sleeps a lot in class.
    - Talks back, sometimes under his/her breath.
    - Will not answer questions verbally but performs well in written work.
    - Has poor personal hygiene and the other students tease him/her.
    - Is very bright and talks out before the others have a chance to think of the answers.
    - Gets up and walks around the room without permission.
    - Does not like the subject you are teaching and he says his dad agrees that it is a waste of time.
    - Is overweight and wears a coat everyday. He is ridiculed by others.
    - Has no friends
    - Doesn't want to go to college in spite of his parent's expectations.
    - Complains to the counselor that the teacher hates him. "Get me out of social studies!"
    - Is failing and the parent blames the teacher for not providing help or teaching.

Al Katz, M.S.

MORE ROLE-PLAY SCENARIOS

PURPOSE: To help participants find role-play subjects and situations.

DIRECTIONS: Choose one of the above or make up a problem on your own. Avoid solving the problem for the client and try to focus on using the Reality Therapy Process.

1. A student is failing due to a lack of homework preparation.
2. An employee is chronically late to work.
3. A friend is unhappy in his/her marriage.
4. A client wants to reduce the stress in his/her life.
5. A friend hates his/her job.
6. A student disrupts the class with his/her class clown behavior.
7. A colleague is afraid to approach the boss about a work-related issue.
8. A friend wants to lose weight.
9. A child can't seem to get ready for school on time.
10. A student cheats on a quiz in you class.
11. An employee is disappointed he or she did not get the promotion that he or she applied for
12. A client wants to quit smoking
13. An employee has trouble meeting deadlines.
14. A student is failing because of low test grades.
15. A friend has a chance to get an exciting new job, but has to move to get it and doesn't want to move

Collected by Brandi Roth, Ph.D.

CREATING ROLE-PLAY QUESTIONS ACTIVITY

PURPOSE: Effective question building can be used to brainstorm ways to focus on the concepts below in a role-play.

DIRECTIONS: Make up or find a question you can ask from each of these categories.

Building Relationship	Exploring the Perceived World	Focusing the Want

Exploring The Quality World	Exploring Total Behaviors	Guiding Self-evaluation

Exploring Options	Creating A Plan	Choosing An Action

Adapted from an activity created by:
M. Patricia Donihee and Ellen B. Gelinas

CREATING ROLE-PLAY QUESTIONS
FOR A LEAD MANAGEMENT ACTIVITY

<u>PURPOSE:</u> Effective question building can be used to brainstorm ways to focus on the Lead Management concepts below in a role-play.

<u>DIRECTIONS:</u> Make up or find a question you can ask from each of these categories or use to record questions as a process observer of role-play.

Building a positive relationship	Connecting habits	Identify basic needs

Open to identifying and addressing concerns	Understands the system	Builds trust

Models Lead Management	Encourages strengths	Emphasizes quality, responsibility, and improvement

Encourages ideas for planning and solution	**Self-evaluation**	**Encourages collaboration, coaching or mentoring**
Clarifies the vision, direction, aim, purpose	**Assesses knowledge & skills**	**Clarifies expectations**
Clarifies the Worker's Motivation (wants)	**Delivers Effective/Helpful External Feedback**	**Encourages workers to learn from each other's skills**

By Brandi Roth, Ph.D., Carleen Glasser, M.A. and Bob Hoglund, M.A.

SAMPLE QUESTIONS ACTIVITY

PURPOSE: Role-play practice

DIRECTIONS: Create a role-play that has at least one question from each category in it. As you do the role-play have an observer write down each of the questions from the list below which were used.

I. Questions to identify specific wants in the quality world.

How satisfied are you with your life? What would your life look like if you were satisfied?

Is what you are experiencing what you envisioned when you were first married?

What would be different if your life was the way you wanted?

How can I help you today?

What would you really have if that happened?

II. What are you doing? (TOTAL BEHAVIOR)
Tell me about a typical day.

What have you done to get what you want?

III. Is what you are doing working? (EVALUATION)
How is that working for you?

Is it helping?

How successful have you been?

Is your behavior what we agreed upon? (or against the school rules?)

HINT:
1. Use questions involving vision and how things look; use few questions which elicit a "yes" or "no" answer. Use the language of the client as much as possible. Accept no excuses.
2. Ask one question at a time then wait for client to answer. Ask for specifics or clarification if the answer is vague.

Compiled by Brandi Roth, Ph.D.
from various training experiences

MORE QUESTIONS FOR ROLE-PLAY ACTIVITY

PURPOSE: Finding alternative ways to ask questions in a role-play

DIRECTIONS: Select one question from each category and create an alternative way of expressing it. Defend your alternative choice to a partner.

Relationship
- What would you like to happen here today?
- What's the problem?
- What is the solution?*
- How would you like your relationship with _____ to be?
- What have you been doing to improve this?
- What would your (our) involvement look like?
- Can I get you something to drink?
- A good joke—funny—"effort to disarm"
- What brings you here today?
- Are you here by your own choice?
- How specifically can I be of help to you?
- Is there anyone else that can help you?
- Who has previously helped you?
- When is the next time I can see you?

Quality World Pictures
- What do you want?
- What are the things in life that are most important to you?
- How can you get these desires satisfied?
- Do you have a plan?
- Who are the people involved in helping you get what you want?
- Have these people been helpful in the past?
- What is preventing you from getting what you want?
- Why is this want so important?
- What wants do you have in your quality world?
- What want is driving the car?
- What are you doing to prevent yourself from getting what you want?

Total Behavior
- Is how you are behaving getting you what you want?
- Is your behavior meeting your needs?
- Who controls your behavior?
- What are you feeling or thinking?
- How is that working for you?
- What are your wants and needs?
- Who is driving your car?
- What concrete thing(s) are you prepared to this week?
- If you were going to do something concrete to accomplish your goal—what might that be?
- If you change your behavior will that change your outcome?

Self-Evaluation/Evaluation
- When you tried talking about it—how did it go? Feel? What feedback did you get?
- Looking back would you do anything differently?
- What have you learned about yourself from this process?
- How will this help you in the future?
- What could you do differently next time to get what you want?
- How did it feel when you got what you wanted?
- How is your situation different now than it was then? What made the difference? What was the benefit?
- What did you learn from this?
- Will this solution be effective for other situations?
- What was ineffective? What was effective?

Creativity/Plan
- What is your plan?
- Have you made a plan?
- What plans have worked for you?
- What would your situation look like in the future?
- What do you need to do to make your plan work?
- What part of your plan can you implement now?
- What could you do if your plan doesn't work out or if you don't do it?
- How will you know if things are working for you?
- What do you see yourself doing, saying, thinking and feeling when you are choosing need behaviors?
- What do you picture yourself doing in 5 years?
- What can I do to help you with your plan?
- Are you going to have to give something up with this commitment?
- What is the need you are addressing with this need?

Collected by Brandi Roth, Ph.D.

SELF-EVALUATION ACTIVITY
WAYS TO PRACTICE ROLE-PLAY ELEMENTS

PURPOSE: This provides a way to look at questions and improve practice of Choice Theory and the process, helping to avoid letting the story become central instead of building experience with Choice Theory. Essentially it is a normal role-play, then changing seats to practice evaluation.

DIRECTIONS: Ask participants to put pairs of chairs facing each other. Tell person on the west side that they are the client and tell the person on east side that they are the counselors

| Counselor | Counselor | Counselor | Counselor |
| Client | Client | Client | Client |

1. Tell each other what kind of person you would like them to be (the role-play scenario) (allow about 2 minutes)
2. Counselor start to counsel this person (allow about 10 minutes)
3. Now stop, and don't speak about it.
4. Clients please stand. Move one seat to the left. The end person moves down and takes the first seat on the other end.
5. Counselors don't tell the story that was discussed with the former client. Your job is to help evaluate the relationship that was just enacted. Do not discuss specifics. Discuss the role-play content. What do you think of using this method of Self-evaluation? What questions contributed to a "change of direction" in the role-play?
6. Clients think of a question that you just asked that had a significant impact on the self-evaluation.
    What different questions could you ask?
    What question did you feel was the best and why?
7. Counselor: What questions were asked that had a significant impact on you as a counselor? (Example: How did you get to know her?)

Debrief: What are you learning about self-evaluation with this activity?

Al Katz, M.S. and Kathy Curtiss

MATRIX FOR HELPING PEOPLE USING CHOICE THEORY; WHAT EVERY ROLE-PLAYER SHOULD KNOW

WHAT WE ALREADY KNOW ABOUT PEOPLE BEFORE WE SEE THEM	WHAT WE NEED TO FIND OUT ABOUT PEOPLE WHEN WE SEE THEM	WHAT PEOPLE NEED TO LEARN THAT WE CAN TEACH THEM
They have 5 basic needs	Which of their needs is not being met	To understand their needs and how to satisfy them
They have a quality world	The specific pictures in their quality world	That they can put pictures in their quality world and can take them out
All their behavior is total behavior	What choices they are making now	That they can only control themselves not anyone else
Their creativity is always working	What their creativity is offering them now	How to use creativity to solve their problems
Their perception of the real world is their reality	The information they are getting from the real world vs. their quality world	How changing their perceptions can help them make better choices
They are unhappy because they have poor relationships caused by the use of external control	Which present relationship they are having trouble with and why they are having trouble with it	What external control psychology is and how using Choice Theory instead can improve their relationships
They spend a lot of time evaluating others' behavior and less time evaluating their own behavior	When and with whom they have self-evaluated and who they are evaluating instead of themselves now	That they will be safe to self-evaluate because they are in a trusted relationship with us
They seldom have a plan for changing their ineffective behaviors to more effective ones	If they would be willing to make a plan to change their own behavior to improve their relationships	How to make a plan that they will be committed to do today to improve their relationships

NOTE: The Role-Play Feedback Sample Questions Form and the Role-Play Feedback Form match the sequence of the information in this Helping People Using Choice Theory Matrix.

Carleen Glasser, M.A.

EXAMPLE
ROLE-PLAY FEEDBACK FORM—SAMPLE QUESTIONS

PURPOSE: A way to record what happened in the role-play by the process observer.

DIRECTIONS: During the role-play write questions you hear the counselor ask in each category below:

BASIC NEEDS QUESTIONS:

♥ Love/Belonging.

> Who loves you? Who do you love?

🦋 Freedom

> What choices do you have?

☺ Fun

> What do you do for fun?

☆ Power

> What do you do that you are proud of?
> Whose behavior can you control? When do you feel in effective control of your life?

Survival

> Do you take risks?
> Are you safe and secure?
> Are you a spender or a saver?

QUALITY WORLD QUESTIONS:

> If you had a magic wand, what would you wish? If your life was like an empty canvas what would you paint on it first?

TOTAL BEHAVIOR QUESTIONS:

> i.e. What are you doing now to get what you want?

Carleen Glasser, M.A.

COMPARING PLACE/CREATIVITY QUESTIONS:

i.e. does what you have match what you want?

PERCEPTIONS QUESTIONS:

Is that a positive, negative or neutral for you?

RELATIONSHIP QUESTIONS:

Do you have a best friend?

EVALUATION QUESTIONS:

Did your actions get you what you want?

PLAN MAKING QUESTIONS:

What can you do today to move in a different direction?

Carleen Glasser, M.A.

ROLE-PLAY FEEDBACK FORM

During the role-play write questions you hear the counselor ask in each category below. Use the spaces provided to write what the counselor asks.

BASIC NEEDS QUESTIONS:

♥ Love/Belonging.

Freedom

☺ Fun

☆ Power

Survival

QUALITY WORLD QUESTIONS:

TOTAL BEHAVIOR QUESTIONS:

Carleen Glasser, M.A.

COMPARING PLACE/CREATIVITY QUESTIONS:

PERCEPTIONS QUESTIONS:

RELATIONSHIP QUESTIONS:

EVALUATION QUESTIONS:

PLAN MAKING QUESTIONS:

Carleen Glasser, M.A.

B.

FOCUS GROUPS AND FOCUS GROUP ACTIVITIES

FOCUS GROUPS

USING FOCUS GROUPS TO TEACH CHOICE THEORY AND REALITY THERAPY

FOCUS GROUPS AS GROUP THERAPY IMPLEMENTED BY COUNSELORS

William Glasser, M.D. introduced Choice Theory focus groups in his *book* ***Warning: Psychiatry Can Be Hazardous To Your Mental Health.*** In 2003 Dr. Glasser creates what he calls a Choice Theory Focus Group in which about a dozen people meet twice a month to discuss how they could put Choice Theory to work in their own lives and help others in the group to put it to work in theirs. It is an easy and enjoyable way to deliver public mental health. He continues to describe focus groups in ***Defining Mental Health As A Public Health Problem; A New Leadership Role For The Helping Professions***

A few counselors or small groups of counselors could get together and offer a public mental health program, and he suggests a Choice Theory Focus Group. These focus groups could be made available to HMOs, public and private counseling services, pain clinics, social service agencies, college and university health services and private physicians. These people are all using the very expensive medical model to treat people for both psychological and medical symptoms not supported by pathology. Counselors could take a leadership role in promoting real mental health and gain much status in the process and offer better mental health directly to the public. Counselors trained in Choice Theory could run the groups and explain how they are using Choice Theory in their own lives.

Dr. Glasser describes how to involve the community in focus groups as education in two of his recent books. ***Defining Mental Health As A Public Health Problem Booklet, A New Leadership Role For The Helping Professions*** and ***Warning Psychiatry Can Be Dangerous To Your Mental Health.***

HOW TO ROLE-PLAY A FOCUS GROUP IN PRACTICUM FOR THE PURPOSE OF LEARNING HOW TO FACILITATE ONE ACTIVITY

Choice Theory Focus Groups as Education in Practicum and Intensive Weeks

The practicum or training group could simulate a Choice Theory Focus Group. After they have enough Choice Theory information have them teach each other some of the pieces they have learned and what they have read. Many of them come having read at least the booklet, ***Defining Mental Health as a Public Health Problem.***

Goals:
- Preparing to use role-plays to facilitate Choice Theory focus groups.
- Focusing on education not group therapy. Like all role-play opportunities it is a vehicle for deepening understanding of Reality Therapy and Choice Theory.
- Practicing working with simulated clients
- Feeling comfortable with the language of Choice Theory
- Practicing the language of counseling and how to use that language effectively
- Learning to take external control out of your own approach to counseling

Have each participant:

1. Select one chapter of the book, ***Warning Psychiatry Can be Hazardous to Your Mental Health***. Read and prepare the chapter for group discussion
2. Make up questions to ask the group based on the selected chapter information which would encourage discussion.
3. Take turns playing the part of the facilitator until each person in the group has had the opportunity to do it once.
4. After the experience ask the group to process the activity by asking them the following questions:
    a. What did you do with your group as you facilitated it that you believe was most useful for learning Choice Theory?
    b. What problems did you encounter?
    c. What would you do differently the next time you facilitate?

Carleen Glasser, M.A.

C.

PRACTICE WITH RELATIONSHIP ROLE-PLAYS:

COUNSELING, HELPING AND LEAD MANAGEMENT

THE FOUR WHEELS GAME
ROLE-PLAY ACTIVITY

PURPOSE: How to role-play Total Behavior using the Four Wheels Game Role-Play Activity.

DIRECTIONS: You need four people to participate. Each person must draw one wheel, like the ones below, on a piece of paper. Decide who will draw the front wheels and who will draw the back wheels. Each person should then stand holding his wheel, matching the wheels below or place chairs in the configuration of a Total Behavior Car. Participants role-play a scenario from the voice or behavior of each wheel. Using round robin apply the *Four Levels of Happiness with Connecting and Disconnecting* and the *Role Play Using Problem Solving Framework*.

MATERIALS NEEDED:
> For this activity you will need the handouts: *Four Levels of Happiness with Connecting and Disconnecting* and *Role Play Using Problem Solving Framework*
> Blank paper, pens and markers
> 4 chairs for each group of participants

First, check to see if your wheels are in the right places. The four players acting out the wheels are all representing one person with a problem or dilemma. Decide as a group what the problem to role-play is and describe it.

Use this activity with any problem you have to help you see it clearly and solve it in Total Behavior terms. Now, state the dilemma then answer the following questions:

Feeling Wheel: Tell us what you are feeling about the problem.

Body Talk Wheel: What is going on inside you? Do you have any symptoms?

Thinking Wheel: What thoughts are on your mind concerning the problem?

Acting Wheel: What are you doing about this problem?

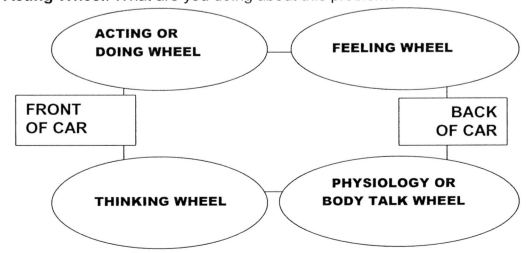

After each wheel talks, decide if the **Car** is going down a road that will help or hurt. If not then revisit the acting and thinking wheels to think of another action that would work better in this situation. Try your new action or plan, and then see how you feel physically and emotionally.

EXAMPLE SITUATIONS:

    Bossy boss
    Not enough money to pay expenses
    Children moving back home
    Family members not close
    Families combined because of marriages
    Frustration getting along with co-workers
    Couples with different needs or behavior

QUESTIONS TO THINK ABOUT:

What am I doing to get what I want?
Whose behavior can I control?
What would be a good choice of behavior for the relationship?

OPTIONAL ADDITIONAL ACTIVITIES:

1. Identify which wheel these questions represent:
    What do you need/want?
    What are you doing? How are you behaving?
    Whose behavior can we control?
    Is it working?
    What assessment and self-evaluation is occurring?
    What is your plan?
    How do you plan, trust your choices? Does creativity ever stop?

2. Rotate positions on the chairs:
    Move places four times to practice being that voice in your own way.
    Symptoms and responses can vary with each person's perception

3. Ending activity:
All wheels are operating simultaneously.
You have shifted from less effective to more effective in your plan.
Have all four wheels voiced their part out loud.

4. Sample scenarios to use in the Four Wheels Activity:

    Workplace Scenarios:
    - Working in a job where no one seems to get along. There is never a "meeting of the minds." What can you do?
    - Working hard and need a vacation, but you have too many bills to pay so you can't afford to take one. What can you do?

- Your boss gave you a poor evaluation at mid-year and you don't know what to do about it because you are doing the best job you can and working very hard at it. You think it is unfair.
- Hospital nurse received a complaint about the care of a patient.

Relationship/Marriage Problems Scenarios:
- You're getting married next week and you have "cold feet". Are you making a mistake? Is he or she the right person for you?
- You want your wife to go to work to help out with the bills but she wants to stay at home with the children.
- Your husband wants to let his mother come and live with you. She is 85 years old and very cranky. You never did like her and really don't want her to move in.
- Affair in the marriage
- You believe you and your wife (husband) have fallen out of love with each other. You have drifted apart and when you are together you hardly talk except to argue.
- Your older daughter and her two children have come back home to live with you and it is destroying your marriage.
- Money issues: Being in debt, avoiding working, gambling excessively, spending problems.
- Coping with challenging behaviors: Controlling family member, someone depressing or panicking, criticizing, threatening,
- Pending divorce and a dispute over custody.

Family, Parent, Child Challenges:
- A student has a ten page report due for school; they are anxious, jittery, sweating, procrastinating, and going out to escape. The paper is finished by the deadline. How does the car drive now?
- Family member's illness and death.

Brandi Roth, Ph.D. and Carleen Glasser, M.A.

FOUR LEVELS OF HAPPINESS WITH CONNECTING AND DISCONNECTING

PURPOSE: The purpose is to understand role play counseling a person with four levels of happiness both connected and disconnected.

DIRECTIONS: Role-play counseling a person from each level using the connecting or disconnecting relationship.

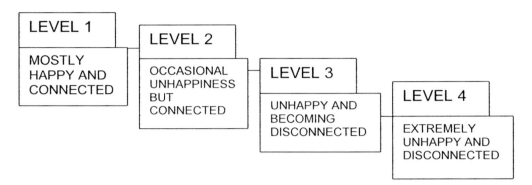

LEVEL 1: Being connected in relationships leads to happiness. Questions to consider: Am I enjoying happiness? Am I making choices that help the relationship? Am I self-evaluating and self regulating (organizing behavior)? Does your quality world match your real world?

CONNECTING IN RELATIONSHIPS WITH: HAPPINESS – LOVE – JOY - ACCEPTANCE LAUGHTER - TRANQUILITY - PEACEFULNESS - PLEASURE - INTIMACY - CONNECTEDNESS

  FEELINGS: Calm, peaceful, secure

  PHYSIOLOGY: Healthy, smiling, eyes twinkling, alert, relaxed body and mind

  THINKING: Focused thinking, more effective choices, calm thoughts, thoughts of self and others, planning and goal setting, loving thoughts, optimism, planning events, secure, accepting, relating with connection, flexible thinking, open-mindedness. Matching pictures of quality world, using caring habits: supporting, encouraging, listening, accepting, trusting, respecting, negotiating differences.

  ACTING: Attached, relating with self and others, living in the present, pursuing interests, follow through with plans, achieving, learning, practicing affinities, working, making good choices, feeling freedom to choose, creative, having fun, stable behavior, adaptable, resilience, organized, making good choices, caring choices, cooperative, self-soothing, attached, flexible with change, responding to vulnerability, learned optimism.

LEVEL 2: Occasional unhappiness but connected. Symptoms arise in normal life. Repetitive thoughts may occur. People choose to blame or act as if the situation is unfair. Instead of seeing choices, people personalize situations. Using Choice Theory provides options to recognize, to acknowledge and to take action! Make choices (thinking and doing). Ask questions to gain more effective control? What did that feel like? What was your physiology? What did you do? Did I have a part in this situation? Did I contribute to the effectiveness or ineffectiveness? What could I do to take action? What are my creative ideas? What are my choices? What is important to me? I can... I will... I need....I want....

DISCONNECTING IN RELATIONSHIPS WITH: UNHAPPINESS - HURTING - SADNESS FEARING – GRIEVING – ANXIETYING - STRESSING - DISTRESSING - FRUSTRATING INJUSTICES - DISAPPOINTING

FEELING: Give and get support, resolve conflict (agreeing, agree to disagree or compromise), organize or able to organize, experience closeness, interdependent, self-sufficient, self-regulating

PHYSIOLOGY: Frowning, furrowed brow, heart fluttering, eyes surveying the environment, slouching, blushing, overly alert, quizzical expression

THINKING: Pondering options and choices, considering choices, weighing options, reflective thoughts, discussing choices, seeking counsel, intense thinking with options, reflective thinking, pictures don't match, reflections

ACTING: Observing other's actions, reflective talking, expressing options, rigid/closed posture, arms folded, and hands in pockets

LEVEL 3: Unhappy and becoming disconnected. Preoccupation with the situations in the past or the future. Recognizing less effective control and the need to return to Level 2 of happiness.

DISCONNECTING IN RELATIONSHIPS WITH: ANGERING – DEPRESSIONING - GUILTING NEED FOR DRAMA - ANXIETING / PHOBIAS – STRESSING - RETALIATION - DESPERATION HOSTILITY - BITTERNESS - HATE - ADDICTIVE BEHAVIORS - HOLDING GRUDGES

FEELING: Shame, guilt, emotional, blame, vulnerable, unhappy

PHYSIOLOGY: Somatic complaints: headache, stomachache, irritable bowel, bladder, body aching, immune system weakness, emotional, crying, pursed lips, sighs, yawns, racing heart, sweating palms, hands clenched, body tense and yawning, flush red, nauseous, despair on face, fatigue, respiration rate elevated

THINKING: Shame, guilt, external control thoughts, intrusive thoughts, worrying, depressing thoughts, scared, unfocused thoughts, stuck in thoughts, restricted thinking and preoccupation, helpless, pessimism, negative imaginings, learned helplessness

ACTING: Restricted or avoidance behaviors, impulsive, activity, distracted at work, passive, angering, depressing, dependent, anxiousness, narrowing the field of choices, weighing options, using the deadly habits: blaming, criticizing, complaining, nagging, threatening, punishing, bribing

LEVEL 4: Extremely unhappy and disconnected. Violence to self and/or to others.

DISCONNECTED IN RELATIONSHIPS WITH: SUICIDAL - DRUG USE - CRIMES DELINQUENCY - RAGE – THREATS - REVENGE - ABANDONMENT

FEELING: Feelings of terror, unhappy, confrontational, high arousal

PHYSIOLOGY: Agitated movements, illness, body cold/hot, body curled, tense, eyes darting, shaking, blood pressure elevated, heart rate elevated, intense sweating, crying, hyperventilating, exhaustion

THINKING: Plotting, little shame or remorse, controlling, terrifying thoughts, hopeless, despairing, brooding

ACTING: Trauma, panic attacks, external control behavior, aggressive, chaotic, planning, harm to self or others, reckless (driving/living), attacking, defending, dismissive, screaming, throwing and breaking things

Brandi Roth, Ph.D.

ROLE-PLAY USING PROBLEM SOLVING FRAMEWORK

PURPOSE: Problem solving framework can be incorporated in all Role-plays where a dilemma is being discussed by telling a story in a sequence that leads to a plan. Gather information and apply three steps: information about what happened, total behavior symptoms and an action plan leading to resolution. Role-play using a conversational exchange gathers perceptions and provides information to meet a quality world picture of needs. Role-play using a conversational exchange gathers perception and provides information to meet a quality world picture of needs and builds a relationship. This framework applies to role-plays between a counselor and a client or anyone resolving relationship conflicts.

DIRECTIONS: Solutions to dilemmas can be resolved following three steps in the chart below. Ask for what you need and want using caring and kindness. Increase effectiveness by self evaluating and using creativity to make a plan to change direction and/or to change behavior. Use these three steps to resolve the dilemma:

Step 1 PAST	Step 2 PRESENT	Step 3 FUTURE
Dilemma: What happened?	**Analysis:** Total behavior symptoms: How do you feel now? What are you thinking now? What are you doing now? What are your body sensations?	**Action:** What can you do next? Accountability plan: Apologize Make a new choice Change a behavior Take responsibility Self evaluate

Multiple steps may be necessary to reach a creative plan for a more effective solution. Use the following five steps to open the dialogue for communication and discussion:
- <u>Agree</u> by talking over the dilemma and making a plan
- <u>Agree to disagree</u>
- <u>Postpone</u> and come back to discuss at a set time in the future
- Reach a <u>compromise</u>
- Use a <u>mediator</u>

Remember to use the "L.A.S.T." Rule when self evaluating:
- **L** — Listen actively watching for facial expressions and emotions.
- **A** — Accept the 10% that you do not like or agree with and tolerate the differences in viewpoints listening for perceptions, needs and quality world pictures
- **S** — Speak only for yourself and accept responsibility for your action
- **T** — Tell the truth

Brandi Roth Ph.D.

COLLAGE ROLE-PLAY ACTIVITY

PURPOSE: Collages are used as a prompt to introduce role-play scenarios. Topic cards provide prompts to introduce each player in the situations.

DIRECTIONS: Create cards with sentences relating the topic and the needs and wants of the players. Rotate the positions so that all members of the group have a chance to play at least one of the people who have a perceived world viewpoint. Read the card and play the role of the person on the card. Make a collage of photos that reflect a topic you would like to explore from the Real World. Role-play cards for each person introduce the perception of that participant. Make four or more cards that describe the people in the relationship and the questions they want to explore in counseling their perceived world viewpoints. These cards are intended to start the counseling role-play.

MATERIALS NEEDED: Collage with pictures of a topic on the card. Cards containing topic sentences introducing the people in the situation and their perceptions of the dilemma. 3" x 5" cards.

Example: General topics:
- Families in conflict about their relationship
- Families disputing about how to spend time together
- Relationship with one partner with a higher need for fun or freedom.
- Collage pictures of museums, travel sites, etc. that explore a need for freedom to travel or for family vacations.
- Family members relating at home.
- People interacting in the workplace.

Example cards describing the family exploring ways to get their needs met.
- Two teenagers need mom to drive them and to be available to pick them up at midnight after their event.
- James, a 48 year old married man, enjoys his work, has success as a CEO in a company, and is happy with one free day on Sunday. He expects his family to be available to spend time with him. His idea of a vacation is staying home for a week relaxing.
- Jane, a 45 year old married woman wants time away from her children and a weekend trip alone with her husband.

Role-play example using collages:
Retell a movie using Choice Theory language. The collage includes movie pictures, movie and story prompts, pictures of different types of movies such as documentaries, chick flicks, violent movies and/or classic movies. Remember a movie that affected your total behavior (physiology, feelings, thinking and acting). Write the name of your movie on a card. Find a partner in the group who is familiar with the movie. Together tell a summary of the plot. As a pair, retell the story acting out the characters using Choice Theory language. Feel free to change the story direction or ending. Pick one or two related scenes or tell a short story of the whole film. Example movies to try include: Wizard of Oz, Casablanca, It's a Wonderful Life, or King Kong.

Adapted by Brandi Roth, Ph.D. from Jean Suffield's Farm Role-play Activity

ROLE-PLAY RELATIONSHIP STORIES AND OBITUARIES FROM THE NEWSPAPER

PURPOSE: To practice role-playing people's stories about their lives. This is a creative way to experience helping or counseling their stories and to introduce ways to practice finding and developing people's stories and scenarios through role-play.

DIRECTIONS: Work in dyads to practice. Role-play an example story from a newspaper article, obituary or magazine relationship story.

"You are a product of your past but you don't have to choose to be a victim of it." William Glasser, M.D.

Choose one of the obituaries from the folder or write your own obituary about someone or read through one of the magazine stories.

Briefly draw or write a summary of the story or the legacy. Note some of the details about the person's life happiness and/or unhappiness. What do you know about how they changed their life? Did they self-evaluate? Did they improve their life? How did their life change? What behaviors appeared unexplored?

Meet with a partner and role-play in a dyad: the story, the regrets, the second chances. Use Choice Theory ideas to change the story.

MATERIALS NEEDED:

      Paper, Pen, Markers
      Collection of obituaries from newspapers
      Relationship stories from magazines or reprints of articles
      3" x 5" cards

Follow-up role-plays:

1. Write down a relationship question you have been pondering to role-play. The situation could be in the workplace, about a friend, a situation at home, or a client dilemma. Take the 3 x 5 card, circulate around and get at least five answers and ideas to resolve the problem using Choice Theory integrated thinking.

2. Introducing role-play practice with a whole group. The facilitator plays a client. The whole group takes turns asking questions and counseling in a round robin.

Brandi Roth, Ph.D.

AXIOMS OF RELATIONSHIPS ACTIVITY

PURPOSE: The purpose of this role-play activity is to focus on a real problem in a relationship.

DIRECTIONS:
1. Discuss how you would teach the following axioms in a role-play. What questions would you ask the client that would lead them to understand this information?

- Golden Rule: Treat others as you would want them to treat you.

- The only person you can control is yourself.

- Internal control empowers the self.

- The less you attempt to control, the more people will do what you want.

2. Discuss the following: A relationship is a "connecting place"

    A place to enter
    A place to leave (time out and individual growth)
    A place to re-enter
    A safe place
    A sacred place

3. Discuss how you would role-play the following ideas:

- What happened in the past that was painful has a great deal to do with what we are today, but revisiting this painful past can contribute little or nothing to what we need to do now. What we need to do now is improve an important, present relationship.

- The inability to handle negative emotions and to solve conflicts causes the deterioration of a relationship.

- Our real world is how we perceive life's situations. Everyone perceives things differently.

Brandi Roth, Ph.D. and Clarann Goldring, Ph.D.

THE LANGUAGE OF CHOICE THEORY ACTIVITY

PURPOSE: To learn how to role-play various situations where the problem is a matter of using external control and not knowing the Choice Theory alternative.

DIRECTIONS:

Using the book *The Language of Choice Theory*, Glasser and Glasser (1999), select a page that has an external control dilemma and create a role-play based on solving the dilemma by teaching the client some Choice Theory language. Use your creativity to help the client think of alternative language to the examples in the book.

EXAMPLE:
1. Select a page from the Parent and Child section
       a. Have the parent as your client and counsel from that point of view.
       b. Have the child as your client and counsel from that point of view

Do the same for all the roles in a page from:
       a. The Love and Marriage Section
       b. The Teacher to Student Section
       c. The Manager to Employee Section

Carleen Glasser, M.A.

RELATIONSHIP TUG OF WAR ACTIVITY

PURPOSE: Developing questions and answers about relationship dilemmas that can be resolved for need fulfillment.

MATERIALS NEEDED:
    4 x 6 Cards
    Pens

DIRECTIONS:
- Take a card
- Think about questions that occur repeatedly in a relationship that you have (Dilemmas)
- Write a specific question about an issue you have in a relationship with a family member or a partner. (You probably know the answer because of your own quality world pictures, needs, or beliefs.)
- Do not write the answer
- Write who the players are at the top (Father-Child/Mother-Child)
- Mingle among yourselves
- Find someone and discuss possible choices for a solution
- Write the solutions that are suggested on the back of the card
- You will be asked to change partners every few minutes to repeat the process
- Keep your questions with you
- Continue to get additional opinions
- In a few minutes we will return to the large group and talk about the solutions you collected
- Debrief the group
    1. What did you like about this activity?
    2. Discuss a variety of perspectives and scenarios
    3. Discuss similarities and the overlap of the dilemmas
    4. Discuss way to make connections
- Remember the needs are universal; pictures are specific

Brandi Roth, Ph.D.
Adapted from Lucy Billings

RELATIONSHIP INVOLVEMENT ACTIVITY

PURPOSE: To focus on relationships and how people choose to participate in them.

DIRECTIONS: Role-play two people in a relationship using the following questions and continuum:

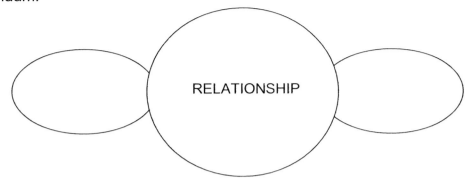

How do you choose to participate in your relationship?

EFFORT

	Little	Moderate	More

CONNECTING   ☐-------☐-------☐-------☐-------☐
                1   2   3   4   5

DISCONNECTING ☐-------☐-------☐-------☐-------☐
                1   2   3   4   5

CONNECTING HABITS: (Circle what you already contribute to your relationship)

SUPPORTING - ENCOURAGING - LISTENING - ACCEPTING – TRUSTING - RESPECTING - NEGOTIATING DIFFERENCES - KINDNESS - COOPERATION - CREATIVITY- CONCENTRATED EFFORT

How else can you contribute positively to your relationship?

_____

_____

DISCONNECTING HABITS: (Circle the habits you use but want to change)

CRITICIZING – BLAMING – COMPLAINING – NAGGING – THREATENING - PUNISHING- REWARDING TO CONTROL – DEFENDING – DEGRADING – SARCASM – STONEWALLING – ATTACKING

How can you choose to remove negativity from your relationship? What is your plan?

_____

_____

Brandi Roth, Ph.D. and Clarann Goldring, Ph.D.
Adapted from *Getting Together and Staying Together* by William and Carleen Glasser

RELATIONSHIPS AND OUR HABITS
ROLE-PLAY ACTIVITY

PURPOSE: The purpose of this activity is to increase awareness of how external control used in relationships is linked to the unhappiness people experience in their lives.

DIRECTIONS: Select one of the disconnecting habits below and create a role-play that deals with one of the three versions of that habit. For example: choose criticizing.

1. Create a role-play in which the client is being criticized by someone in his/her life and show how the client can learn to deal with the criticism using Choice Theory.
2. Create a role-play where the client is the one doing the criticizing and show how to teach a new way to behave, based on self-evaluation, using Choice Theory.
3. Create a role-play in which the client is criticizing him/herself and has trouble completing tasks or has difficulty making new relationships.

In each role-play be sure to emphasize the impact each version of the habit is having on the client's relationships.

In each role-play be sure to include how a connecting habit can be used to replace the disconnecting habit being used. For example: *Criticizing* another can be replaced by *Accepting*.

SEVEN DISCONNECTING HABITS
1. Criticizing
2. Blaming
3. Complaining
4. Nagging
5. Threatening
6. Punishing
7. Bribing or rewarding differences to control

SEVEN CONNECTING HABITS
1. Supporting
2. Encouraging
3. Listening
4. Accepting
5. Trusting
6. Respecting
7. Negotiating

Carleen Glasser, M.A.

THE SOLVING CIRCLE

Key Principles

- There are three players in our Solving Circle: **you, me** and **our relationship**
- We agree that **our relationship is more important** than what we want as individuals
- We agree to **be gentle with each other** when inside our Solving Circle
- We agree to **negotiate** and look for ways to **compromise**
- We agree to **look for things we can do** to help our relationship

The Solving Circle Principles are based on ideas by Carleen & William Glasser in their books: *Choice Theory: A New Psychology of Personal Freedom* & *Getting Together and Staying Together*

ROLE-PLAY SOLVING CIRCLE ACTIVITY

PURPOSE: To role-play couples using the structured Reality Therapy Solving Circle.

DIRECTIONS: The group should face each other in two rows of equal number.
Row 1 -- Chair 1 – Partner A
Row 2 -- Chair 1 – Partner B

Activity 1. Partner A: Ask a question to increase the effective connection with each other. Spend five minutes with Partner B dialoging about a need (Love and Belonging, Power, Freedom, Fun and Survival).

- With one minute warning wrap up and prepare to move to next partner and ask the same questions.
- Now reverse chairs and Partner B asks a question of Partner A.

Activity 2. A relationship dilemma should be decided upon between Partner A and Partner B. The facilitator asks the following questions of each partner.

1. Are you here to get help for your marriage?
2. Whose behavior can you control?
3. What do you think is wrong with your marriage to _____?
4. Tell me what is good about your marriage to _____?
5. Tell me something you could do to help your marriage?

Brandi Roth, Ph.D. and Clarann Goldring, Ph.D.

ROLE-PLAY WITH A NEED STRENGTH PROFILE

PURPOSE: To create interesting clients to role-play with different personalities.

DIRECTIONS: Create a role-play using the following Need Strength profile. Ask your participants to fill in the following numbers on this profile: 1, 3, 4, 5, 4. How would you counsel someone with the need strength profile of 1-3-4-5-4? What kind of personality would this client have?

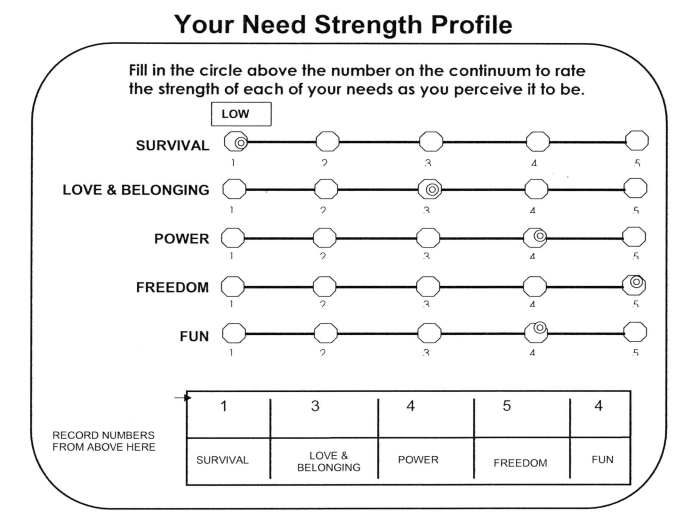

The following page provides additional Need Strength Profile forms for this activity.

William Glasser, M.D. and
Carleen Glasser, M.A.

Make up other need strength profiles on the form below and role-play a client from them:

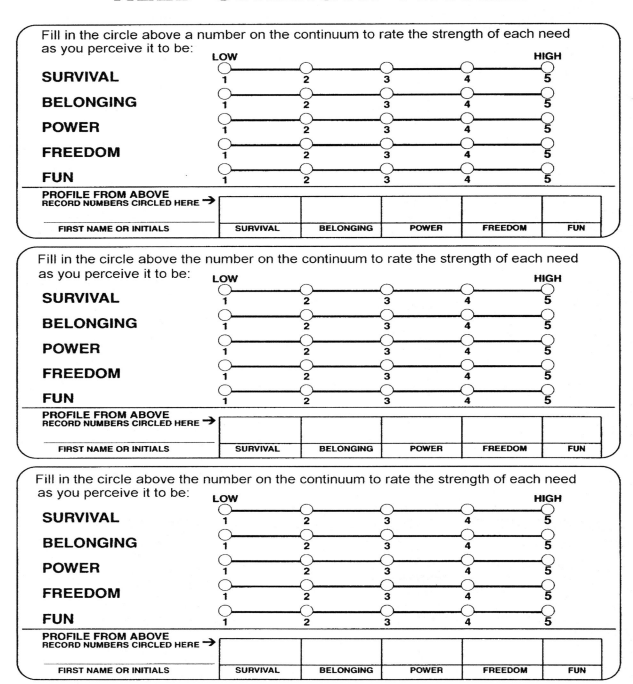

CHOICE THEORY ROLE-PLAY
USING THE SHIFT PROCEDURE

PURPOSE: The purpose of this activity is to increase knowledge and skills in counseling and/or Lead Management through successive exposure to different ways of approaching each role-play. Individuals in the roles of counselors and lead managers have an opportunity to experience three different ways in which a situation might be presented and can put their knowledge of Choice Theory into practice. Individuals in the roles of clients and employees have an opportunity to experience three different styles of counseling and Lead Management that might be applied with the same individual. The purpose of the debriefing is to reflect on what each participant learned as a result of shifting.

DIRECTIONS: Participants divide into pairs and choose the role of counselor or client (in a counseling role-play) or manager or employee (in a Lead Management role-play). A single vignette is provided to all participants. Participants spend 10 minutes--or an alternate period appropriate to the educational situation--enacting the role-play. After ten minutes, the individual playing the client (or employee) shifts to a different counselor (or lead manager) and re-enacts the role-play, from the beginning, for an additional ten minutes. Following the initial role-play and two shifts (a total of 30 minutes in the same role), the group debriefs the experience.

Depending on the group's needs and the time available, an additional vignette can be provided at the conclusion of the debriefing. Participants can choose new roles and repeat the shift procedure for an additional 30 minutes, followed by another debriefing.

It might be that on any given round one of the counselors or lead managers does not have a partner, e.g., because the group has an odd number of participants. If possible, the solo individual should follow the most recent client/employee to the next role-play and observe the same individual's interactions with another counselor/lead manager.

Jeffrey Tirengel, Psy.D, M.P.H.

CHOICE THEORY ROLE-PLAY USING THE SHIFT PROCEDURE: SHOBA'S COUNSELING SITUATION

Shoba, age 16, has been extremely agitated for the past two weeks. She has been up most of the night nearly every night. A junior in high school, she has been unable to concentrate or to sit through her classes. On two occasions she has left school during the day because of her high level of distress. She has been irritable with her family members and peers, unable to eat, and reports "not feeling or acting like myself." This is your first meeting with her.

This is a significant change from Shoba's previous behavior. Shoba has been an honors student and always done well with her peers and her teachers. She denies any history of substance abuse. Her friends are among the most successful academically in the high school, and all are college-bound. Most are aiming for prestigious universities, and the high school has an impressive record of admissions to the most competitive academic institutions. Some have begun to prepare for the Scholastic Aptitude Test which they will take a few months from now during the spring semester. Others have begun visits to universities and colleges throughout the United States and have started making decisions about where they will apply.

Shoba has recently broken up with "my first serious boyfriend," a break-up that he initiated. She has also recently experienced the death of her uncle (her father's brother, age 52), who died suddenly from a heart attack. This was the first death to a person close to Shoba.

Shoba's parents, who were raised in India, brought the family to the U.S. seven years ago. They both have professional degrees and expect the same of Shoba and her younger brother, age 13.

Shoba wants counseling to help with "whatever is going on with me."

Jeffrey Tirengel, Psy.D, M.P.H.

CHOICE THEORY ROLE-PLAY USING THE SHIFT PROCEDURE: HAROLD'S LEAD MANAGEMENT SITUATION

You are in charge of custodial services in a large public elementary school. The recently-arrived principal has told you that Harold, one of the two custodians whom you supervise on-site, has been yelling at teachers. According to the teachers, Harold says their classrooms are "too messed up at the end of the day." The teachers have also told the principal that Harold has been yelling at groups of children when he finds that the bathrooms or other parts of the school grounds have been, in Harold's terms, "trashed."

You have been working with Harold for many years, and similar reports have surfaced many times. You know that Harold takes pride in his work and tries to do a good job. However, he is quick to anger and quick to yell, especially when he thinks that others are being disrespectful to him or to school property.

Harold is nearing the age when he could retire, though he will not get maximum benefits because he has not been working in the school system long enough. He has never been married, and he lives alone. Harold regards you as one of his only friends, and he has told you in the past that "you are the only one who understands me." Harold knows that you are planning to leave at the end of the school year to be closer to your elderly parents in the Midwest. He has also told you that he is worried about who will replace you as his supervisor, and he is not sure what to do when you leave.

Harold is the youngest of 21 children, most of whom are no longer alive. Harold has told you that his mother "used to bank my head against the wall" as a form of discipline. Harold had minimal education and can barely read. His only pleasures outside of work are watching movies and riding his bicycle.

At the principal's direction, you are meeting with Harold to discuss his most recent angry outbursts. She has told you that continued outbursts of this kind could result in Harold's dismissal.

Jeffrey Tirengel, Psy.D, MPH

D.

QUALITY WORLD ACTIVITIES

MY QUALITY WORLD RELATIONSHIP ACTIVITY

PURPOSE: This activity can be used in dyads to practice processing relationship information and to increase awareness of what couples say and do and how they express what is in their quality world and how they get their needs met in the relationship. This can demonstrate ways they are compatible or incompatible. When they are incompatible with pictures that do not match this it can harm the relationship. Pulling the rubber band gives a physiological sense of tug of war.

DIRECTIONS: This activity would be facilitated in a practicum as a role-play activity. Provide each dyad with two rubber bands. Participants form partnerships. They will be role-playing two people in a relationship. Using two rubber bands tied together to form two loops with a hole in the center, discuss what you want in your quality world to satisfy your needs for survival, love and belonging, power, freedom and fun. As you tell each other your wants, pull your side of the rubber band so that the knot is over your own quality world circle. If you both have the same want or picture, the hole will stay in the center space where the circles overlap. The more the hole remains over the overlapping space, the stronger the relationship. (See diagram below.)

You have two quality worlds in a relationship.
This is mine (one rubber band); this is yours (the other rubber band)
When we choose to come together, we tie them together to form the relationship we share:

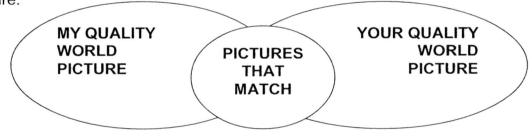

The more we widen what we share the more we get along.

When one person pulls for what they want the Quality World changes. If you pull the Quality World apart and if you keep pulling it will break. If you want something and it hurts the relationship your partner will pull back. Role-play the ideas of the Quality World pictures that are important to you. Example situations might include tolerance for choices or imperfections or differing needs. A third person then steps in to counsel the couple.

The role-play leads the person playing the counselor to open dialog for a series of questions such as: What were you thinking? What were you feeling? How was your body responding? What action were you taking? What did you need? What were you doing? How is this helping or hurting your relationship? How do you communicate with one another? What is this doing to your relationship? What kind of habits did you use? Were they connecting habits or disconnecting habits?

Carleen Glasser, M.A.

SAMPLE QUESTIONS ABOUT MY QUALITY WORLD PICTURES ACTIVITY

PURPOSE: Once one identifies their quality world pictures the role-play has a goal.

DIRECTIONS: Develop additional questions that you can ask the client to specifically identify what is in his or her quality world. Write these questions in the spaces below or have clients fill in the boxes after each category with their wants.

CATEGORIES	SATISFIED PICTURES	YET TO BE SATISFIED
PEOPLE	WHO DO YOU HAVE IN YOUR QUALITY WORLD WITH WHOM YOU ARE IN A GOOD RELATIONSHIP?	WHAT KIND OF RELATIONSHIP DO YOU WANT? WHAT DOES THAT RELATIONSHIP LOOK LIKE?
THINGS OWNED OR GENERAL	WHAT IS IN YOUR QUALITY WORLD THAT IS VERY NEED SATISFYING?	WHAT ARE YOU LOOKING FOR TO SATISFY YOUR NEED FOR _____?
SYSTEMS OF BELIEF	WHAT DO YOU BELIEVE IN THAT MATCHES A PICTURE IN YOUR QUALITY WORLD?	WHAT IDEAS DO YOU WANT TO LEARN MORE ABOUT TO GET YOUR NEEDS MET?

Carleen Glasser, M.A.

QUALITY WORLD PICTURES: THE "P" PRINCIPLE

PURPOSE: Quality world pictures are made up of people, places, things and systems of belief. All pictures in our quality world are need satisfying. Using caring and connecting habits is the quickest way to build trust. Thinking of the letter "P" helps us to recognize our pictures of a quality world of happiness and connected relationships.

DIRECTIONS: Pair together with someone you do not know well in the group. Fill in your Quality World Pictures. Share parts or all of your Quality World with your partner.

A **PLACE** in my quality world that when I am there it is need satisfying is _____. A **PERSON** in my quality world that when I am with them I meet my needs is _____. A **POSSESSION** I have that is need satisfying is my _____. Something I **PARTICIPATE** in that meets my needs is _____ and _____ something that brings me **PEACE** is _____.

Something I **PRACTICE** that is need satisfying is _____ and something I am very **PROUD** of is _____. I also meet my needs by practicing the **PRINCIPLE** _____ as I live my life.

A **PASSION** I have is _____ that helps me to meet my needs. A group of **PEOPLE** that I meet my needs with are _____, A **PEAK EXPERIENCE** that was very need satisfying was _____. A **PET** I had or have that is in my quality world is/was _____.

Something that is **PRINTED** that is in my Quality World is _____ and something that is **PRICELESS** to me is _____. A **PROMISE** that is very important to me that I work hard to keep is _____ and a **PAST EXPERIENCE** or event that is in my Quality World is _____.

Of all the above "Ps", the one that meets my needs the most is _____.

The oldest "P" above is _____ and the newest "P" above is _____.

Brad Greene, Ed.D.

ROLE-PLAY WITH QUALITY WORLD MAPPING ACTIVITY

PURPOSE: Quality world mapping was developed by Suzy Hallock-Bannigan. The quality world is your picture of what is important to you. Quality world topics are generally easy for participants and clients to discuss. They help to build connections in relationships. The activity is unique because the pictures that result can be modified in subsequent sessions or adapted as the counseling progresses by changing, rearranging or removing Post Its as the needs are satisfied.

DIRECTIONS: The quality world mapping role-play activity can be set up with pairs or with a whole group. Use two different color Post Its to show which needs match or overlap. Write the need, perception or want on the Post It. Post Its are then arranged on the paper around the central dilemma (similar to the way webs or mind maps are arranged). Example: a father and daughter unhappily living together. Each person writes what they want or need in this situation on a different color Post It. The Post Its can then be moved or arranged in order of importance to the individual.

MATERIALS NEEDED:
Large supply of Post It Notes in multiple colors (1 ½" x 2" or 3" x 3")
Chart paper or Foam Board (for a large group demonstration)
Colored Paper (This represents the Quality world)
8 ½ "x 11" paper (for individuals role-playing)
Pens and Markers

DESCRIPTION: Different situations can be counseled using this technique. This activity is a vehicle to teach Quality World Pictures and Basic Needs. Discuss what is in your quality world. Formulate questions about quality world: What is your viewpoint? What is your perception? What are your needs? What are your wants? These are the pictures that are important. These are the pictures that are unique to the person. This is a way to communicate your picture and your perceptions to a partner, family member, friend or counselor. This activity provides an opportunity to review differences in learning styles. People learn by doing, by seeing, by hearing (auditorially), by feeling and by drawing.

Quality World topics that are easy to talk about include: vacations, cars, food, clothes, sports, beverages, possessions, films, tools, people in quality world, family, getting along, and dilemmas to solve. EXAMPLE: Jan chose the topic of Food. We made a Quality World Picture of her view about food. This provided a safe vehicle for her to begin to discuss her viewpoint about a familiar topic.

Family Relationships: Getting along, resolving conflict, facing situations that are unresolved.

Quality World Mapping by Suzy Hallock-Bannigan, RTC, CAGS
Adapted by Brandi Roth, Ph.D.

COUNSELING SESSION EXAMPLE OF A ROLE-PLAY USING QUALITY WORLD MAPPING

This is an example of a quality world mapping during a counseling session involving a father and daughter stating their needs and wants for a connected happy living together relationship. Each person used different colored Post It notes to write what they wanted to get their needs met. Subsequent sessions referred to the map for progress adjustments and changes of needs.

Reunion
What would you like for:
Greetings
Departure

Maturity
Body Changes
Gynecological appt. (women)
Health plan

How can Dad be helpful (useful) to you?
How can you be helpful (useful to Dad?

Love & Belonging
Fun
Freedom
Power Survival

How to talk about your day. Inquiring minds want to know how you are doing. How can that be asked of you?

Menu planning
Food
Activities
Fun

What do you expect about...?
What would you like to be informed about?

Family Relationship: Father—Daughter (Connecting)

Calendar & scheduling family activities and individual activities

What kind of privacy do you need?

What would make the relationship together happier for you?

Respect
What tone of voice helps with respect?

What would you like your brothers and sisters to understand about you?

What would you like to do to help with household? What would you choose as your way to help?

Tutors meeting with counselors, with Dad, alone or together

Rewards or incentives
What would you like as a reward for completing a task.

Brandi Roth, Ph.D.

E.

QUALITY SCHOOL ACTIVITIES

ROLE-PLAYING CLASS MEETINGS

INTRODUCTION: The reason we do role-play practice with the class meeting format is because many teachers take our training and teachers need role-play experience developing and practicing how to conduct a class meeting.

Also for those counselors who work with small groups or even larger groups of people doing Choice Theory Focus Groups or any kind of group counseling, the class meeting format of Define, Personalize and Challenge is very effective in helping people explore new ideas and develop new skills. It would be very useful for all trainees to have this experience in the role-play segment of their practicum training.

Class meetings were originally introduced in the book *Schools Without Failure* by William Glasser, M.D. in 1969. It is also further described in his more recent book *Every Student Can Succeed*, 2001. There is a kit for teachers called *Class Meeting Flashcards, Choice Theory for Elementary School Students* developed by Carleen Glasser in 2004. The important thing to know about this kit is it not only teaches teachers how to do a class meeting but the purpose of this class meeting is to teach Choice Theory to the students. The teachers learn to understand Choice Theory and they learn how to teach it using this kit. It has a two fold purpose, the teaching of Choice Theory and the social skills development experience that they provide for their students participating in the class meetings.

There are many benefits for the students participating in class meetings. This is a way for students to role-play, using different scenarios for problem solving. Topics include respecting, problem solving, competence, understanding needs, the difference between external control and Choice Theory, the seven deadly habits, the behavioral car, creativity. Every concept in Choice Theory is covered. There is even a section on character and what good character involves.

- **WHY TEACH CHOICE THEORY?**

Choice Theory will help students learn how and why people make choices. With this basic understanding students can discover how to resolve conflicts and improve their relationships with each other. They will learn a life skill that will give them the tools to unlock the mystery of how to get along better with the people around them and to find the happiness that comes with making effective choices in life. Each of the topics for class meetings included in this set is designed to teach a different Choice Theory concept. For continuity it is important to cover these topics in sequence.

- **WHAT IS A CLASS MEETING?**

Based on the Glasser Quality School ideas developed by William Glasser, M.D., a class meeting is an intellectual discussion in which students can express their opinions and learn new information. In a class meeting all students sit facing each other in a circle or oval and as each student gives his or her opinion on a topic or question proposed by

- **HOW IS A CLASS MEETING ORGANIZED?**
    1. The role of the teacher is to **select a topic** for the discussion and ask specific questions about the topic.
    2. The students are asked first to **define** the topic.
    3. Next, the students are asked questions that help them to **personalize** the topic.
    4. The students are then asked questions that **challenge** the topic personally or globally
    5. Finally, they are given an assignment to do at home.

The questions asked for each topic are merely guidelines for you to follow. If you think of additional questions, feel free to use them. The only suggestion is to make the questions open-ended requiring more than a "yes" or "no" answer. You may wish to focus on specific information in your curriculum, as it seems appropriate to the topic of the meeting. Co-relating Choice Theory ideas with the subject area content make it more relevant to the curriculum and a richer learning experience for students. The time frame of the class meeting is up to you to determine. It can be as brief as ten minutes, but it is recommended that you end it sooner rather than later. Keep the students involved, interested, and asking for more.

Carleen Glasser, M.A.
Class Meeting Flash Cards
Choice Theory for Elementary School Students

THE ART OF QUESTIONING
IN CLASS MEETINGS

Define the topic so all have the same understanding. Use "What is…?" "What are…?" type questions e.g. "What is a leader?" "What does it mean to evaluate yourself?" "What is external control?"

Personalize the questions to your group, situation or life. Questions should include the word "you" or "your". For example: If you were the leader, what would be the first change you would make? Do you like to be evaluated or do you prefer to evaluate yourself? Who controls you?

Challenge questions should create a thought-provoking situation to stimulate thinking, creativity and imagination. Use questions such as: What if…? Where would…? And/or How would…? What if we didn't have a leader? What is the true purpose of self-evaluation? How does external control affect relationships?

    Look for new angles or play devils advocate
    Examine assumptions and look for relationships
    Probe rather than skim the surface
    Avoid exhausting a topic or working toward closure

Questions for the group
    Tell your partner how you get close to someone
    What contributes to a group being perceived as fun?
    When do you feel important in a group?
    How can a group leader give choices to participants?
    What factors contribute to safety in a group?

Al Katz, M.S.

CLASS MEETING GROUP ACTIVITY

PURPOSE: Group role-play activity to teach a teacher or participant how to facilitate a class meeting. Build listening skills, build conversation skills, have an opportunity to say opinions, feelings, or needs; create relationship experiences and connection opportunities.

DIRECTIONS: The group sits in a circle. Each person takes a turn facilitating the class meeting following the format below.

Format for class meetings:

1. TOPIC:
    Pick a topic

2. DEFINE:
    Define a topic to discuss
    What is…..? (example, communication)
    One person can speak at a time
    (There are no right or wrong answers)
    (All views are respected)

3. PERSONALIZE:
    What is your personal experience with this topic?
    How important is it to you?
    What are other people's needs?
    What are other people's reactions?
    What are your reactions?
    Your viewpoint?

4. CHALLENGE:
    Challenge the topics with other viewpoints
    What if you lived in an external control world?
    What if we lived in your world with restricted communication?
    Character education?
    Ideas vs. opinion?
    What is external control? When is external control effective and ineffective?
    What are choices?
    How are needs met?
    What needs do you have that have not been discussed?

Compiled by Carleen Glasser, M.A. from various sources

Appendix of Supplementary Information

ESSENTIALS OF CHOICE THEORY

<u>What is Choice Theory?</u>

Choice Theory attempts to explain both the psychological and physiological behavior of all living creatures. It maintains that all we do from birth to death is behave, that our behavior is internally motivated and chosen, and is our best attempt to satisfy one or more of our basic needs built into our genetic structure: survival, love and belonging, power, freedom, and fun. In practice, the most important need is love and belonging, as closeness and connectedness with the people we care about is a requisite for satisfying all of the needs.

Dr. Glasser offers Choice Theory to replace the present external control psychology that almost all people in the world use – trying to make another person do what we want them to do. This forcing, punishing psychology is destructive to relationships, and when used will destroy the ability of one or both people to find satisfaction in that relationship. It will also result in their becoming disconnected from those with whom they want to be connected.

Disconnectedness is the source of almost all human problems such as what is called drug addiction, violence, crime, school failure, spousal and child abuse and marriage breakdown to mention a few. With Choice Theory, we can change our thinking and replace deadly behaviors with ones that help us move closer to those with whom we work and live.

The ten axioms of Dr. Glasser's approach are found in his book, *Choice Theory: A New Psychology of Personal Freedom*. Teaching Choice Theory is an integral part of all Institute programs. The ten axioms are as follows:

1. The only person whose behavior we can control is our own.
2. All we can give or get from other people is information. How we deal with that information is our or their choice.
3. All long lasting psychological problems are relationship problems.
4. The problem relationship is always part of our present lives. We are free to live happily when we have at least one satisfying personal relationship.
5. What happened in the past that was painful has a great deal to do with what we are today, but revisiting this painful past can contribute little or nothing to what we need to do now: improve an important, present relationship.
6. We are driven by five genetic needs: survival, love and belonging, power, freedom and fun.
7. We can satisfy these needs only by satisfying a picture or pictures in our quality worlds. What we choose to put into our quality worlds is the most important.
8. All we can do from birth to death is behave. All behavior is total behavior and is made up of four inseparable components: acting, thinking, feeling and physiology.
9. All total behavior is designated by verbs, usually infinitives and gerunds, and named by the component that is most recognizable. For example: angering or depressing.
10. All total behavior is chosen, but we have direct control over only the acting and thinking components. We can, however, control our feeling and physiology indirectly through how we choose to act and think.

What is Reality Therapy?

Reality Therapy is the method of counseling that Dr. Glasser has been teaching since 1965. It is now firmly based on Choice Theory and its successful application is dependent on the counselor's familiarity with, and knowledge of, that theory. In fact, teaching Choice Theory is now part of Reality Therapy. Since unsatisfactory or non-existent connections with people we need are the source of almost all human problems, the goal of Reality Therapy is to help people reconnect. This reconnection almost always starts with the counselor/teacher first connecting with the individual and then using the connection as a model for how the person can begin to connect with the people he or she needs.

Reality Therapy is different from most psychotherapeutic approaches because it focuses on the present and helps people understand that they can choose a better future. This is based on the Choice Theory axiom that states, regardless of what has occurred in the past, to be happy and effective we must live and plan in the present. Because of this, it is an effective, short-term, therapy in the age of managed care.

To practice Reality Therapy, we create trusting relationships with clients. From these relationships, we are usually able to help them evaluate both what they want and the total behaviors that they are presently choosing. We then assist them in creating a plan to either change what they want to something more achievable, and/or to choose behaviors that will better satisfy what they now want.

What is Lead-Management?

The William Glasser Institute also works extensively with organizations, such as schools, to replace external control theory with Choice Theory as the psychology that drives the system. In practice, this means moving from a boss-management approach to one of lead-management.

Lead-managers continually work on the system to create a non-coercive environment within which students/workers can self-evaluate and achieve quality work. The only way any organization will achieve quality work is if the lead-manager can persuade students/workers to continually upgrade the system by communicating in ways that build trust. The work and effort from employers is always useful work.

What is a Quality School

The Glasser Quality School Training Program is based on the concepts first described in Dr. Glasser's book, *The Quality School*, and later in his 1998 book, *Choice Theory: A New Psychology of Personal Freedom* and *Every Student Can Succeed*. The program is geared towards helping individual schools create the necessary systemic change that can lead to the creation of a Glasser Quality School.

In this process, the role of the principal, utilizing Lead Management principles, is crucial to the process. Once the staff is committed to the vision of crating such a school and has begun to facilitate change in the learning environment, intensive week training is provided. Dr. Glasser has outlined six criteria to achieve the designation of a Glasser Quality School. Once the principal believes the school has met that criteria and is ready to declare, he/she directs a letter to Dr. Glasser.

To qualify as a Quality School six criteria are required:

1. Relationships are based upon trust and respect, and all discipline problems, not incidents, have been eliminated.
2. Total Learning Competence is stressed and an evaluation that is below competence or what is now a "B" has been eliminated. All schooling is defined as useful education.
3. All students do some Quality Work each year that is significantly beyond competence. All such work receives an "A" grade or higher, such as an "A+".
4. Students and staff are taught to use Choice Theory in their lives and in their work in school. Parents are encouraged to participate in study groups to become familiar with Choice Theory ideas.
5. Students do better on state proficiency tests and college entrance examinations. The importance of these tests is emphasized in the school.
6. Staff, students, parents, and administrator view the school as a joyful place.

The six conditions of Quality School work:

1. There must be a warm, supportive classroom environment. A strong friendly feeling among teachers, students and administrators encourages trust. Together they must believe that the others have their welfare in mind. Students are encouraged to talk honestly and openly without coercion.

2. Students should be asked to do only useful work. Students understand the work that is assigned to them. Memorizing is minimized.

3. Students are always asked to do the best they can do. Quality work requires time and effort and students are given sufficient time to make the necessary effort.

4. Students are asked to evaluate their own work and improve it. Quality can always be improved and quality work is encouraged. Students self-evaluate their own work. Quality takes precedence over quantity.

5. Quality work always feels good. Students experiencing the work and parents and teachers observing the work feel good. Personal achievement through hard work is need satisfying.

6. Quality work is never destructive. The environment is safe and free of addictive drugs or anything destructive.

William Glasser, M.D.

Conditions for Quality in a Quality School
As Applied To Role-play Self-evaluation

Quality Schools are unique in their approach to building relationships between students, teacher, parents and staff. All Quality Schools use a rubric for connecting students with each other and the adults involved in their learning to build a relationship and success.

Students learn role-play, solving circles, and class meetings and feedback as ways to increase connection and build relationships. Faculty, students and parents are aware of the conditions of quality in a Quality School.

1. Always useful
   - How will the information you have benefit the student now or in the future?
   - If "in the future" how can you ask the student to do homework in a way that feels good today?
   - No personal criticism. Give feedback as information.

2. Atmosphere of Friendliness
   - Feels good to self and others
   - Needs satisfying
   - How can you address the needs of the group to set the environment? (Love & belonging, Power, Freedom, Fun, Survival)

3. Best Work
   - Help the student define quality work (They need a clear picture to target)
   - Each student should complete at least one piece of work that you both agree is quality before passing a course.
   - Discuss with the student the benefits of doing quality work.
   - Remember the source of motivation/behavior: To get what we want which satisfies our needs.

4. Conditions of Quality
   - Always Useful
   - Our Best Effort
   - Continuous Improvement
   - Never Destructive
   - Self Evaluate
   - Feels Good

Notes from William Glasser Lectures

CHOICE THEORY GLOSSARY OF TERMS

BASIC NEEDS:	The genetic instructions which we are constantly attempting to fulfill: Belonging, Power, Freedom, Fun and Survival
BEHAVIORAL SYSTEM	The system through which we create all of our behaviors, constantly creating and reorganizing as well as storing regularly used behaviors.
COMPARING PLACE	Where we compare what we want (Quality World Pictures) with our perception of what we're actually getting
FRUSTRATION SIGNAL	The actual electrical/chemical signal which activates our behavioral system, felt as an urge to behave
NEW BRAIN:	Psychological needs, learning, writing, higher order functions
OLD BRAIN:	Controls automatic physiological functions--breathing, heartbeat, etc.
PERCEIVED WORLD	All we know: our perception of reality; total memory
PERCEPTUAL SYSTEM	The system through which we filter information coming in from the real world
QUALITY WORLD	What we want the most—the people, places, situations, and things that have satisfied our needs, strong emotion, connected. Source of motivation
REAL WORLD	The people, situations, and things that actually exist
SENSORY SYSTEM	First filter of information from the real world: sight, hearing, taste, touch, smell
TOTAL BEHAVIOR	All behavior is total and made up of four components: Acting, thinking, feeling and physiology. May be effective or Ineffective. All behavior is purposeful—to act on the world to get what we want which satisfies our needs
TOTAL KNOWLEDGE FILTER	Everything we've perceived without negative or positive values or feelings
VALUING FILTER	The filter through which we compare information with what we want

William Glasser, M.D., Adapted by Al Katz, M.S.

THE ECONOMICS OF CHOICE THEORY FOCUS GROUPS AS GROUP THERAPY
William Glasser, M.D.

As explained in the booklet, *Defining Mental Health as a Public Health Problem*, Choice Theory offers a solution to one of the most puzzling of all human problems: **how to get along much better with each other than we do now**. We could do this by making Choice Theory focus groups available at either low cost to individuals or free as a part of a widespread public mental health program as described in the booklet.

But also, as explained in the booklet, there could be much opposition to the public mental health model from both the psychiatrists who prescribe brain drugs and the powerful pharmaceutical industry that makes and promotes them. There are huge rewards in money and prestige for psychiatrists to continue to use the medical model. There are no rewards for any of the other mental health professionals such as psychologists, social workers, and counselors who along with a few psychiatrists like myself do not prescribe. To the contrary, there is also both active and covert opposition from these psychiatrists and the pharmaceutical industry to the counseling and psychotherapy we do.

I believe the best chance we have to overcome this opposition is for mental health professionals who counsel and teach to join me in pointing out what the continuing use of the medical model is costing our whole society both in untold individual misery and in unbelievable amounts of tax dollars.

The Costs Implicit in the Medical Model

For individuals, the failure of sexual relationships both with and without marriage and the wide fallout from this failure in family problems is by far the greatest source of human misery. In our society, we spend hundreds of billions of tax dollars on a failing attempt to improve education, billons more to control crime (we have essentially given up on rehabilitating criminals) and countless billions to treat pain, fatigue and weakness which have no pathology to explain those symptoms. All of the money spent can be easily traced to a single source: human beings who want to get along better with each other but have yet to figure out how.

We Can't Solve This Problem if We Don't Accept Its Existence

It is the almost universal acceptance of the medical model that has led to our inability even to recognize that the core problem is our failure to get along with each other to the extent we want. Instead we are led by physicians including psychiatrists who believe that our inability to get along is caused by pathology in the brain even though there is not a shred of scientific evidence to support this belief. Based on this false belief they continue to prescribe brain drugs and worst of all tell these countless unhappy people they can do nothing to help themselves.

Using The Public Mental Health Model There Is Both A Lot We Can Do And No Shortage Of People Who Can Help Us Do It.

First, we have to recognize that getting along better with each other is a public mental health problem, not a medical problem. Second, even with all the shortcomings of the medical model under which they are forced to operate to make a living, almost all psychologists, social workers and counselors have still managed to effectively counsel individual clients to help them resolve problems with their marital partners, children, parents, families and other people in their lives. While some of them have learned to counsel using Choice Theory--my method of counseling—most, who are not familiar with this theory, use other theories equally well.

But if we would revisit all the unhappy people in the external control world in which we all live, it would be obvious that even if we were liberated from the medical model, we would still not be able help these huge numbers by counseling them individually. Fortunately, any mental health professional who wants to teach Choice Theory focus groups can be easily trained to do this by the faculty of The William Glasser Institute. These focus groups are a good example of how to deliver public mental health. When they meet they will discuss either my 2003 book, *Warning, Psychiatry Can be Hazardous to Your Mental Health* or my 1998 book, *Choice Theory.*

Learning Choice Theory in these small groups is completely voluntary. People can learn as much as they want and everything they learn will help them to get along better with the important people in their lives. In this instance a little learning can do no harm. The main incentive to learn more is from the theory itself. The more it is learned the better and quicker it works. It does not require any special educational background and it is both easy and pleasant to learn. It is also both politically and religiously neutral. Not one of these sectors has ever voiced any concern with these ideas.

Start a Practice by Teaching Choice Theory Focus Groups

The first worry that crossed my mind when I started my practice in 1956 was where I would I get clients. I got most of them from the women who worked at the desk of the UCLA out-patient clinic where I trained. At that time UCLA charged ten dollars an hour and I told them I would see anyone in my office for that amount as well. From that start I built a small practice and since I was soon writing, consulting and teaching I didn't need more.

If you are starting out with a group or in a clinic under licensed supervision you would not need a license to start a Choice Theory focus group if your supervisors were willing to follow your progress as you teach the group. That way you could share with your supervisor what you are doing and could be the person who gets this process going in the organization or clinic.

When starting such a program it is very important to explain that this is not group therapy. It is a class that learns Choice Theory together by discussing the booklet and either the book, *Choice Theory* and/or the book *Warning, Psychiatry Can Be Hazardous to Your Mental Health*. Since the topic of marital problems often comes up in these groups they may want to go on to my book that explains how to put Choice Theory to work in their marriage, *Getting Together and Staying Together.* You can charge what you want for the groups but my advice is keep the cost low to start with. You can always raise the price if the market will allow.

Some Choice Theory focus groups that are already in progress are experiencing success dealing with pain management, domestic violence, drug addiction, parenting, recovery from divorce, relationships with teens, problems in the workplace, senior citizen challenges, reliance on psychiatric drugs, working with inmates, teacher team-building groups, and people on waiting lists at mental health centers. Many of these groups include people from more than one of the categories listed above and this diversity often increases the effectiveness of the group.

It is not necessary to be seriously unhappy to join a Choice Theory focus group. People who want to experience personal growth and improve their well being are also welcome. How a focus group forms and gets started is described in detail in the book, *Warning, Psychiatry Can Be Hazardous to Your Mental Health*.

Assuming that you get your focus group together and you have a license to counsel, many HMO's now cover a certain number of group therapy sessions and it is very likely that people in the group will not only want group work, but will also desire individual counseling. As soon as this happens you should be on your way both as a counselor and a teacher of public mental health and a group therapy specialist.

About The Authors

Brandi Roth, Ph.D.

Brandi Roth, Ph.D., is a Licensed Psychologist in private practice in Beverly Hills, California. Her counseling practice specializes in relationship issues between adults, children and families. She counsels academic and behavioral problems and provides comprehensive neuropsychological evaluations. She provides client advocacy to facilitate optimum school placement and monitoring through interaction with school staff and other professionals.

Dr. Roth holds a Ph.D. degree in Counseling Psychology, specializing in marriage, family and child counseling, as well as teaching credentials. Dr. Roth previously worked in education as a regular and special classroom teacher, educational therapist, administrative specialist and in-service instructor. Her educational experience encompasses classroom teaching and program administration as well as staff development, in-service training, consulting, and lecturing. She is a consultant to therapeutic and educational organizations in the public and private sectors. Dr. Roth's seminars train other therapists and educators in counseling techniques, behavior management, and compensatory strategies for individuals with differing learning styles and special needs.

Dr. Roth is the co-author of two books with Fay Van Der Kar-Levinson, Ph.D. Her book *Choosing the Right School for Your Child,* is a nationwide guide and workbook for families selecting elementary and secondary schools for their children. *Secrets to School Success, Guiding Your Child Through a Joyous Learning Experience* guides families through the adventures of elementary, middle and high school life. This book provides practical tools to encourage families to have an effective and joyous school experience. She has also co-authored *Relationship Counseling with Choice Theory Strategies* with Clarann Goldring, Ph.D. This book presents tools and tips to guide couples and individual clients toward successful and happy connections using Choice Theory and Reality Therapy strategies. Techniques are directed toward counselors working with the dynamics of relationship happiness, toward other teaching venues and toward everyone using practical strategies for connecting and closeness in everyday life. A problem solving framework provides steps to resolving dilemmas. The program interactively and experientially presents both theoretical and practical approaches. Participants learn to assess relationships and the levels of behaving, to understand the impact of past relationships on the present relationship and ways to self-evaluate.

Dr. Roth is a William Glasser Institute faculty member and Basic Intensive Week Instructor. She presents at The William Glasser Institute International Conferences. Dr. Roth is a co-founder of Dr. Mel Levine's Los Angeles Schools Attuned program, a program to teach awareness of learning differences to teachers and children. She is on the national Schools Attuned faculty and a member of the Los Angeles Schools Attuned Advisory Board. Further information is available on her website at www.associationofideas.com.

Carleen H. Glasser, M.A.

Carleen Glasser, M.A. has twenty-five years experience in education, twelve of which were as a school counselor, specializing in group work with all ages using her extensive training in substance abuse counseling and Reality Therapy. She has taught at the college level, both on and off campus at the college of Mt. St. Joseph and Xavier University. She has been a Senior Faculty member of The William Glasser Institute since 1994 and presently serves on the Legal Board of Directors of that Institute. As a senior instructor she has taught Basic and Advanced Intensive Weeks and Basic and Advanced Practicum sessions at the Glasser's home since 2000.

Mrs. Glasser has worked with her husband, William Glasser, M.D. teaching his ideas all over the world. She served as a presenter at the Milton Erickson Foundation Evolution of Psychotherapy Conference, American Counseling Association Conference, Connecticut Counselors Association, Alfred Adler-Adlerian Conference in Vancouver, B.D., Michigan Counselors Association, Marriage and Family Counseling Association in San Francisco, CA, Memphis, Tennessee Foster Parents Association, Idaho Correctional Counseling Association in Boise, Idaho, South Carolina Counseling Association and North Carolina Counseling Association. Outside of the United States she has presented in Dublin, Ireland, Tokyo, Japan, Zagreb, Croatia, London, England, Seoul, Korea, Lake Bled, Slovenia, Modena, Italy, Oslo, Norway, Australia and New Zealand.

Recently she has been appointed to the Council for the Human Rights of Children and spoke at a symposium on Counselor Education at Oxford University in Great Britain. She has done numerous presentations at the International Conference of the William Glasser Institute.

Her books and activities, which teach Choice Theory to children, have been used in many countries besides the U.S. and have been translated into the Korean, French, German, Hebrew, Croatian and Russian languages. She has co-authored three books with Dr. Glasser, *The Language of Choice Theory, What Is This Thing Called Love?* and *Getting Together and Staying Together*, all published since 1999.

Since 1995 she has helped Dr. Glasser by editing his nine most recent books and offering creative suggestions in the design and graphics of these books. She has also appeared with him in several professional audio and videotapes produced for educators, counselors, and married couples.

Mrs. Glasser's mission is to promote Choice Theory and all its applications to help people learn to live happier, healthier and more productive lives.

Recommended Resources And References

RECOMMENDED RESOURCES AND REFERENCES

An extensive list of all resources dealing with Reality Therapy and Choice Theory by various authors can be found on The William Glasser Institute Website.

CONTACTS:

William Glasser Institute Website: www.wglasser.com

Carleen Glasser, M.A. and William Glasser, M.D., 22024 Lassen Street, Suite 118, Chatsworth, CA 91311, (818)700-0506, (800)899-0688, E-mail: wginst@wglasser.com, Website: www.wglasser.com

Brandi Roth, Ph.D., 433 N. Camden Drive, Suite 1128, Beverly Hills, CA 90210, (310)205-0615, Fax (310)275-3885, Website: www.associationofideas.com

ADDITIONAL REFERENCES:

Jean Seville Suffield, *A Role-Play Notebook: Questions That Really Make A Difference,* E-mail: jeanseville@hotmail.com, Website: www.choice-makers.com

Robert Wubbolding, Ed.D., Website: www.realitytherapywub.com, (513)561-1911

ROLE-PLAY HANDBOOK

UNDERSTANDING AND TEACHING THE NEW REALITY THERAPY, COUNSELING WITH CHOICE THEORY THROUGH ROLE-PLAY

WRITTEN, COMPILED AND EDITED
BY

Brandi Roth, Ph.D.
433 N. Camden Drive, Suite 1128
Beverly Hills, CA 90210
(310)205-0615
www.associationofideas.com

Carleen Glasser, M.A.
22024 Lassen St., Suite 118
Chatsworth, CA 91311
(800)899-0688
www.wglasser.com

Brandi Roth, Ph.D. is a psychologist, consultant, educator, author and faculty member of The William Glasser Institute. Her books, including *Choosing the Right School for Your Child, and Secrets to School Success; Guiding Your Child Through a Joyous Learning Experience*, co-authored with Fay Van Der Kar Levinson, are guidebooks for parents through the process of school selection and school life. She co-authored *Relationship Counseling with Choice Theory Strategies* with Clarann Goldring, Ph.D. Dr. Roth specializes in relationship counseling.

Carleen Glasser, M.A. is an educator, school counselor and a senior faculty member of The William Glasser Institute. She currently teaches Choice Theory throughout the world with her husband, William Glasser, M.D. She *co-authored three books with Dr. Glasser, The Language of Choice Theory, What Is This Thing Called Love? and Getting Together and Staying Together*. Her mission is to promote Choice Theory and its applications to help people learn to live happier, healthier and more productive lives.

ROLE-PLAY HANDBOOK, UNDERSTANDING AND TEACHING THE NEW REALITY THERAPY, COUNSELING WITH CHOICE THEORY is designed for faculty members teaching William Glasser's theories on Reality Therapy, Choice Theory, Lead Management and Quality Schools.

Association of Ideas
PublIshIng
Beverly, Hills, California
www.associationofideas.com

$15.00
ISBN-10: 0-9647119-2-3
ISBN-13: 978-0-9647119-2-1